THE INTERSECTIONS OF FAMILY VIOLENCE AND SEXUAL OFFENDING

Often examined separately, this timely volume provides a detailed exploration of the nexus between family violence and sexual offending. Recognising family and sexual violence as highly interrelated issues, it uncovers the challenges and paradoxes of addressing them as separate versus coinciding problems. What is lost and gained when we treat family violence and sexual offending according to the same framework?

Light is shed on the nature and dynamics of offending; various terminology (e.g., domestic abuse, intimate partner violence, grooming, coercive control); political and policy contexts; myths and misconceptions; policing and investigative responses; children as overlooked victim-survivors; and the punishment and treatment of offenders. Drawing on international literature, case studies, and stakeholder interviews, the book encourages critical consideration to inform future policy, practise, and research, ultimately prompting stronger approaches to reflect victim-survivors' realities and needs.

The book is relevant to the work of professionals in the social service and criminal justice sectors (e.g., police, policymakers, social workers, advocates, and counsellors), and will be of key interest to researchers and students in diverse academic fields such as criminology, forensic psychology, social work, and socio-legal studies.

Gemma Hamilton is a lecturer in criminology and justice studies in Melbourne, Australia. Her research focuses on violence against women and children, with expertise in family violence, sexual offending, policing, and investigative interviewing.

Patrick Tidmarsh is a criminologist and forensic interview advisor, who has worked in the field of sexual offender treatment, with both adults and adolescents who sexually offend, for 20 years. He took the knowledge gained from that work into policing, developing the Whole Story methodology of sexual crime investigation. He trains and lectures on understanding and investigating sexual crime, in Australia, and worldwide.

ROUTLEDGE STUDIES IN CRIME AND SOCIETY

Oppressed by Debt
Government and the Justice System as a Creditor of the Poor
Edited by Saul Schwartz

A Criminological Biography of an Arms Dealer
Yarin Eski

The Rise of Politically Motivated Cyber Attacks
Actors, Attacks and Cybersecurity
Tine Munk

Fieldnotes on a Study of Young People's Perceptions of Crime and Justice
Scaffolding as Structure
Avi Brisman

Violence
Situation, Speciality, Politics and Storytelling
David Wästerfors

Motherhood, Respectability & Baby-Farming in Victorian & Edwardian London
Joshua G. Stuart-Bennett

The Intersections of Family Violence and Sexual Offending
Gemma Hamilton and Patrick Tidmarsh

For more information about this series, please visit: www.routledge.com/Routledge-Studies-in-Crime-and-Society/book-series/RSCS

THE INTERSECTIONS OF FAMILY VIOLENCE AND SEXUAL OFFENDING

Gemma Hamilton and Patrick Tidmarsh

Routledge
Taylor & Francis Group
LONDON AND NEW YORK

Cover image: Getty Images

First published 2023
by Routledge
4 Park Square, Milton Park, Abingdon, Oxon OX14 4RN

and by Routledge
605 Third Avenue, New York, NY 10158

Routledge is an imprint of the Taylor & Francis Group, an informa business

British Library Cataloguing-in-Publication Data
A catalogue record for this book is available from the British Library

Library of Congress Cataloging-in-Publication Data
A catalog record has been requested for this book

ISBN: 978-0-367-50888-3 (hbk)
ISBN: 978-0-367-50885-2 (pbk)
ISBN: 978-1-003-05165-7 (ebk)

DOI: 10.4324/9781003051657

Typeset in Bembo
by Newgen Publishing UK

CONTENTS

ACKNOWLEDGEMENTS

This book has been at least five years in the making. The idea was first born in conversations with Narelle Goodland and Dr. Antonia Quadara. As soon as the book proposal was approved, the COVID-19 pandemic hit, so we have many people to thank for helping us to write this volume during trying times.

First and foremost, we would like to thank the stakeholders who generously offered their time and invaluable insights to inform this work: Sharon Simon, Rachael Burgin, Rebecca O'Donnell, Shureeka Alves, Sarah Hill, Narelle Goodland, SR, and anonymous × 5. It is clear you are passionate about improving practise and responses in these fields and your hard work does not go unnoticed. We would also like to thank the victim-survivor advocates whose quotes and stories we often drew upon to illustrate topics in this book. We really hope this work helps to improve systems, so that healing, justice, and prevention are better achieved. We are also appreciative of Jessica Findling for her research assistance with one of the chapters.

On a more personal level, I (Gemma) want to thank my mum and dad, especially Julie, for all her help with cleaning, cooking, and child-minding so I could get some writing done, especially when childcare centres were shut! To my husband, Chris, thank you for listening to me talk constantly about this book and for your continual encouragement and support. And to Hugo and Adelaide, my sweet little beans, thank you for bringing me so much joy. I love you endlessly.

Patrick's acknowledgements. Firstly, I would like to thank Gemma, without whom this book would never have been written. I would also like to thank everyone who is working to end family violence and sexual offending, to help victim-survivors, or hold offenders to account. It is through your work that we are finally beginning to see significant progress in preventing and responding to these destructive (and endemic) behaviours. Finally, I'd like to thank my partner Jacqui who, as one of those people working on these issues, is a constant source of inspiration, and is a particularly passionate advocate for maintaining the hard-fought gains in responding to those impacted by sexual offending.

ABBREVIATIONS

ALRC	Australian Law Reform Commission
IPSV	Intimate partner sexual violence
LGBTQIA+	lesbian, gay, bisexual, transgender, queer, intersex, and asexual
VAWA	Violence against Women Act
VLRC	Victorian Law Reform Commission

INTRODUCTION

The rates of family violence and sexual offending are staggering, occurring in every country and community around the world. In the United States, for example, a person is sexually assaulted every 68 seconds (RAINN 2022), and across the world, approximately one in three women have experienced physical and/or sexual violence in their lifetime (WHO 2021). Both forms of abuse have garnered unprecedented attention in recent years, but their intersecting nature is often not well understood.

Family violence and sexual offending are frequently, but not always, related. There are unique differences as well as key areas of overlap: (i) family violence that does not involve sexual offending, (ii) family violence that involves sexual offending, and (iii) sexual offending that occurs outside of a family context. About 30–40% of sexual assaults occur within the context of family and domestic violence, although this rate is likely to be higher if you include intimate partner sexual coercion, discussed further in Chapter 1 (ABS 2020; Bagwell-Gray, Messing, & Baldwin-White 2015). Victim-survivors of family violence, as the term indicates, are abused by people they know—intimate partners, immediate or extended family members. Victim-survivors of sexual offending are also typically abused by people they know. Perpetrators are often intimate partners and family members but there are also broader relationships between perpetrators and victim-survivors (e.g., friends, acquaintances, colleagues) and in some cases they may be complete strangers. The latter cases usually receive the most attention in the public arena.

In this book we aim to pull apart the different aspects of family violence and sexual offending and explore how they intersect, largely in the context of social and criminal justice policy and practise. We consider the potential advantages and disadvantages of using "family violence" as an overarching framework to encompass sexual offending. What are the concerns when we only look at these interpersonal harms and victim-offender dynamics through a "family violence" or "sexual

DOI: 10.4324/9781003051657-1

violence" lens? Are there missed opportunities to ensure the safety of child and adult victim-survivors? What is lost and gained when we treat family violence and sexual offending according to the same framework? Ultimately, this book aims to explore the impacts of conceptualising and responding to family violence and sexual offending as separate versus coinciding constructs, with the hope of strengthening future policies and practises.

This introductory chapter begins with a comment on terms used throughout the book. It then explores the nature of family violence and sexual offending, with a focus on key similarities and differences between offenders and victim-offender dynamics. Finally, we turn to an overview and rationale of subsequent chapters.

Terms in this book

We tend to use the terms perpetrators, offenders, and victim-survivors for readability but acknowledge people's identities are broader than what they have experienced or behaviour they have engaged in. We frequently use the term victim-survivor to recognise that people may identify as victims and/or survivors during or following abuse, but in some cases other terminology may be more appropriate. Many people who have been subjected to violence and abuse have not survived. Indeed, one woman is killed by a man every three days in the United Kingdom (Femicide Census 2021). Some women are murdered by men they do not know, like Jill Meagher, an Irish woman living in Australia who was raped and murdered by a stranger while walking home from a pub in 2012. Others, like Indigenous woman Kwementyaye Murphy, are murdered by their intimate partners after suffering years of abuse. Some girls and women, like Americans Audrie Pott and Daisey Coleman, die by suicide following the aftermath of their sexual assaults.

It is important to also recognise that many people do survive family and sexual violence and come up with resourceful ways to endure abuse. Some academics have highlighted that depictions of victims should signal their strength and resilience rather than only portray them as broken and weak (Maher & McCulloch 2020). Grace Tame, survivor of child sexual abuse and Australian of the year in 2021, proudly declared in her winning speech:

> Together we can redefine what it means to be a survivor. Together we can end child sexual abuse; survivors be proud, our voices are changing history. Eleven years ago, I was in hospital; anorexic with atrophied muscles, I struggled to walk. Last year I won a marathon. We do transform as individuals. And we do transform as a community. When I first reported, I was shamed and ridiculed by some. But now my truth is helping to reconnect us. I know who I am, I'm a survivor.

But we also have to critically question who the term survivor is being used for. Author of memoir and manifesto "Is Rape a Crime?," Michelle Bowdler (2020), believes that non-victims may preference the term rape survivor to address their own discomfort with rape victims and trauma. She challenges the binary notion that one must either be irreversibly damaged to be taken seriously, or totally victorious to be publicly acceptable. Here we see Bowdler, "refusing to be either a meek victim or feelgood survivor. She insists on having the gravity of rape and the fullness of herself acknowledged" (Donegan 2020). We hope that use of the term victim-survivor encompasses the continuum of identities and journeys of those who this book is ultimately dedicated towards. The terms family violence and sexual offending will be discussed in depth in Chapter 1.

Sex offenders and family violence perpetrators: Are they one and the same?

There are many similarities between sexual offending and family violence. Both are defined by the relationship between perpetrator and victim-survivor, rather than the offending acts alone. They usually occur behind closed doors, are under-reported, and are both difficult to investigate and prosecute. There are also some significant differences in the profiles of offenders, the impact on victims, reporting practises, as well as policing and criminal justice responses to victim needs. Each area is policed differently, creating unique investigative challenges, particularly as sexual offending entails an exclusively forensic process, whereas family violence may elicit a wider variety of responses, such as the use of intervention orders, or referral to safe housing and other services.

In the early days of sexual offender research, assumptions were completely different, and the premise was that sexual offenders were unlike other offenders, more specialised and fixated, and unlikely ever to desist, particularly those who offended against children. Over recent decades it has become increasingly clear that many of these early assumptions were wrong. For example, Gene Abel's landmark study of child sexual offenders discovered almost one in five reported raping adults, a crossover of offending previously thought unlikely. Later research has confirmed that sexual offenders are much more likely to be generalists than specialists, will crossover age and gender in their offending, and may commit a range of other offences (Abel et al. 1987). Importantly, this includes offences of family and relationship violence. Despite the mass of research in the last four decades, there remain many community myths and misconceptions of both sexual offending and family violence, contributing to the stagnation of effective responses, whether criminal justice, therapeutic, or preventative.

Understanding the offenders

Although the primary goal of all our efforts should be to provide better responses for victim-survivors, offending starts with offenders, so it is important to understand them: Who they are, what they do, how and why they do it, and the impact they have on others, particularly those they offend against.

At the core of our understanding are several acknowledgments. Firstly, that sexual offending and family violence are relationship-based crimes, and both are highly gendered. Most sexual offenders are male and those victimised mostly women and children (ONS 2018; Tarczon & Quadara 2012). Males make up about 20% of those sexually offended against, with the majority abused in childhood (ABS 2017; Dorahy & Clearwater 2012; ONS 2018). Although the figure of 5% has been consistently quoted for the percentage of female offenders, there are some researchers who suggest this may be higher (Cortoni, Babchishin, & Rat 2016; Stemple, Flores, & Meyer 2017). At least 20% of all sexual offences are committed by children and young people, with the majority male here too (Becker et al. 1993; Hackett 2014).

Whilst family violence is also predominantly perpetrated by men, the figures are not as stark. In other words, men are more likely to experience family violence than sexual crime (AIHW 2021). This is, in part, explained by the breadth of family violence perpetration definition, and the narrower scope of sexual offending. Family violence includes psychological and emotional abuses, particularly in the developing focus on coercive control, as well as physical assaults. Sexual offending, despite potential charges for grooming offences, allows little scope for responding outside the physical acts themselves. Even grooming charges must prove the ultimate intention of the perpetrator was a physical, sexual, act.

When it comes to the offences themselves, sexual offenders, particularly those who sexually abuse children, may perpetrate without resort to physical violence, although force and coercion are common. They are more likely to be motivated by the illusion of a "loving" relationship, whereas family violence perpetrators may be more motivated by the desire for power and dominance. There are, however, as Abel's study first demonstrated, many crossover points. Researchers agree that relationships where physical violence is present, will be likely to include sexually abusive acts against adults (Bidarra, Lessard, & Dumont 2016).

There is an increasing focus on children as not just witnesses to adult violence, but also victims of the violence themselves (Bedi & Goddard 2007; Herrenkohl et al. 2008; Hamby et al. 2010). Attention is also turning towards the link between familial violence and child sexual abuse, suggesting children in homes where there is violence are far more likely to be victims of sexual abuse than children who grow up in homes without violence. Some have put the co-occurrence figure of family violence and child sexual abuse as high as 40% (Appel & Holden 1998; Turner, Finkelhor, & Ormrod 2010).

There is also significant convergence in the backgrounds of family violence and sexual offenders. All perpetrator groups have higher rates of familial violence, sexual abuse, and neglect victimisation in their backgrounds than the general population (Bard et al. 1987; Craissati & Beech 2004; Simons, Wurtele, & Durham 2008). Within perpetrator types, however, there may be greater incidences of different abuses, suggesting risk factors to particular offending patterns. Child molesters and rapists, for example, both have high rates of sexual abuse and violence in their backgrounds. However, child molesters have higher rates of child sexual abuse, whereas rapists have higher rates of family violence and physical abuse (Dhawan &

Marshall 1996; Jespersen, Lalumière, & Seto 2009; Seghorn et al. 1987; Simons et al. 2008). Despite these similarities, research is becoming increasingly clear that there are multiple and distinct pathways to each type of perpetration, requiring specific understandings of individuals' offending behaviour to investigate, prosecute, and respond adequately, particularly in determining appropriate treatment and prevention strategies.

In assisting specialist sexual crime investigators to understand offender psychology, motivation, and behaviour, we have utilised the implicit theory (IT) model. The concept of IT derives from the notion that human beings, particularly children, are acting as scientists in the way they explore the world, developing an understanding of their own beliefs, needs, and wants. Early researchers defined the exploratory process as "theory of mind," suggesting that it helped children create theories and beliefs about how to navigate the world, supported by ways of thinking.

IT was first used to study sexual offending by researching the attitudes and beliefs of child molesters. The theory was then tested on rapists and female perpetrators, allowing for a model that was easily understood by investigators across all the major offence patterns they were likely to come across. It is important to note here that typologies and classifications of offenders are a guide only, and that not only do family violence perpetrators sexually abuse, and sexual offenders use coercion and violence in their offending, but that all groups may abuse either adults, or children, or both. Crossover of age and gender is far more common than once believed. It is also important to note that ITs have mostly studied abusive behaviour in heteronormative relationships, where the perpetrator was male and the victims were women or children. It may be that different theories are present where abuses occur in LGBTQIA+ relationships. Having given those caveats, as IT has now been modelled with classifications of sexual offenders and family violence perpetrators, it offers a clear picture of the similarities and differences between the different offender groups.

The first implicit theory studies, looking at child molesters, found that they held five key theories about the way the world works:

- *Dangerous world* refers to the way child molesters perceive the adult world to be a hostile and dangerous place, both psychologically and emotionally.
- *Entitlement* relates to how offenders express their belief that, contrary to societal standards, they are entitled to have sex with children.
- *Uncontrollability* concerns the belief that the world and their actions are uncontrollable and that expression of their "entitlement" is unavoidable.
- *Children as sexual objects* details the construction of children as sexual beings, not only capable of deciding to have sex with adults, but also of initiating those interactions.
- *Nature of harm* refers to the way child molesters justify their behaviour, minimising the harm caused, particularly if no physical force was used.

As these theories were then used to study rapists, females who commit sexual offences, and later family violence perpetrators, it became clear that there was a core set of beliefs that were remarkably similar across groups, but also some notable differences. Family violence perpetrators were found to have a notably broader set of beliefs supporting their offending. The additional theories included beliefs that their behaviour was acceptable and linked to how "real men" behave, that control needed to be maintained and policed, and that violence was provoked, creating grievances and the need for revenge (Gilchrist 2009; Weldon & Gilchrist 2012). None of these latter theories were significant in the beliefs of sexual offenders, whether child molester or rapist.

Connecting all sexual and family violence offenders were the themes of normalising their behaviour and diminishing their responsibility. Unsurprisingly, given the context of patriarchy and the gendered nature of all these crimes, entitlement was significant across all crime themes but one: Female offenders—perhaps pointing to compelling commentary about social learning (Beech et al. 2009).

All perpetrator types believe, or persuade themselves, that men's behaviour, particularly sexual behaviour, is uncontrollable. There are also connections between sexual and family violence offenders in their objectification of those they abuse. Sexual offence theories centre more on the sexual availability of potential victims, and their entitlement to abuse. Family violence perpetrators' theories centre more on the perceived acceptability of their behaviour against women whose behaviour they can believe justifies violence against them. This theme is carried on, in different ways, by all types of offenders, in interpreting the behaviour of victims for their own ends. Child molesters persuade themselves that children desire them sexually, rapists that they know what women want, or deserve, without communication, and family violence offenders that women provoke men's actions.

The difficulties of navigating adult relationships are another consistent theme, although the responses are different, with child molesters retreating into validations of their attraction to children, family violence perpetrators focusing on the need for control and fear of rejection, and rapists believing that women are both dangerous and unknowable, rendering adult relationships futile and doomed to failure. Power is also expressed differently, with child molesters preferring to believe that relationships are mutual and equal, even that they are the victims of children's advances. Rapists believe several variations of the power dynamic, with only one typology focused on taking power as revenge (Knight 1999; Ramirez et al. 2015).

Whilst control is the overall aim of family violence perpetrators, the theme of revenge is more common than in rapists. Finally, there is a unifying theme in that all offenders diminish the damage they do, persuading themselves that no harm was done, and that the behaviour was wanted, deserved, or even initiated. This theory is particularly strong in child molesters, who must navigate much more clearly defined social mores and laws about their behaviour to justify the sexual abuse of children. Each of these theories is supported by a series of cognitive distortions, providing the patchwork that comes together as unique sets of attitudes and beliefs, with varying emphases on each of the implicit theories. In short, the distortions may differ, depending on the type of offender and how they justify their behaviour, but whatever distortions are used will come together as a developing world view, justifying their behaviour.

Grooming versus coercive control

Sexual offenders and family violence perpetrators are connected by core beliefs and theories, albeit with different shades and emphases, but how similar is their behaviour? The two concepts that have dominated the literature researching these two groups are that of "grooming" for sexual offenders, and "coercive control," exhibited by family violence perpetrators. Grooming may be defined as the processes and practises sexual offenders use to develop power and control over those they wish to abuse, overcome any resistance to sexual behaviour, and ensure victims maintain silence and secrecy about the abuse (Craven et al. 2006; Tidmarsh, Darwinkel, & Powell 2012). Grooming has two distinct, and connected, phases, which may be separated as "grooming 1" and "grooming 2." Grooming 1 is the phase of non-sexual grooming, and it is the most important part, providing vital information that investigators may elicit, which may explain what took place and why victims behaved as they did. There may be witnesses to certain elements of the process, even if they did not know about the offending itself. The offender's grooming process also tells us what kind of relationship he believed he had with the victim. It will show what he thought and felt about his offending, and how he justified it, which will be useful to investigators in police interviews, and to therapists who may later work with him in treatment. Once offenders have created a position of power, control, or authority over their intended victim, they begin to sexualise the relationship, which forms the second grooming process.

Coercive control is seen as the process, practises, and tactics that family violence perpetrators use to limit the freedoms of, and exert control over another person, typically a relationship partner (Stark 2006). Rather than a specific focus on sexualising the relationship, as in grooming 2, coercive control may be exerted over a wide variety of tactics, including emotional, psychological, and monetary impacts, as well as sexual and physical harms. There is an argument that sexual abuse, where it occurs in the context of relationship violence, is a perpetrator "tactic," and part of the wider agenda of control and dominance, rather than acts with a singular goal. All sets of offenders will target, or create vulnerabilities in intended victims, before engaging in coercive control or grooming tactics. The starkest difference in these two concepts is that, for sexual offenders, grooming is a means to an end, although they may also derive satisfactions from the processes and practises of the grooming they employ. Coercive control, on the other hand, is an end in and of itself, with additional satisfactions in the variations of strategy and, whilst coercive control research often mentions grooming strategies, grooming commentary seldom includes coercive control. Therefore, not only are there significant variations in the motivations and practises of offenders, the core concepts defining the abusive processes they employ have some considerable differences. In assessing the different tactics and motivations of offenders, and the intertwining nature of family and sexual violence, consider these three stories, taken from real cases:

Case study 1

Determined to stay in control of his partner and children, and to have his wishes followed in all matters, a family violence perpetrator limited access to other family and friends, controlled the family's finances, including having his partner forward all her wages into his accounts, and installed tracking devices in her phone and car. Without recourse to physical violence, his partner cooperated with all sexual requests, despite these being always on his terms. She believed that her submission to him saved both her and the children from violence and felt unable to escape.

Case study 2

A man is charged with multiple counts of sexual abuse and family violence offences, against his partner and children. Evidence of both sexual and violent behaviour is introduced in trials assessing one or the other type of behaviour—that the sexual offending was relevant in the familial violence, and vice versa. After initial conviction, the case is appealed on the grounds that the introduction of such evidence, particularly evidence of sexual abuse in the trial for violent behaviour, was both irrelevant and prejudicial. It was argued that the two behaviours should not be connected. Perhaps surprisingly, at that time, the appellate judges disagreed, considering the evidence relevant as it spoke to "the states of minds of the complainants," and why they both submitted to the abuse and remained in relationship with the perpetrator.

Case study 3

This man had no such compunction about getting what he wanted. An elder in his community, with ties to the local church, this offender decided that he would sexually abuse his daughter, forming a variety of justifications to himself, including that she was a "worldly" child, and that his wife seldom wanted sex, leaving him dissatisfied. After the first occasion in which he abused her, to teach her what was expected, he repeatedly beat and kicked the family dog, in front of her, to ensure her silence.

Although motivations and behaviours differ, showing the breadth of sexual offender and family violence perpetrator typologies, the core of their behaviour patterns is similar. What is also clear is that they have similar effects on victims.

The experience and needs of victim-survivors

As we have discussed, men are typically the perpetrators of family violence and sexual offending, with women and children disproportionately targeted. Crucially, the intersections of sexual and family violence also highlight the terminology of "intersectionality," with those outside the dominant community groups more likely to experience abuse (e.g., women with a disability, Indigenous women, and women from non-English speaking backgrounds: Boxall, Morgan, & Brown 2021). They are also far less likely to report to police and less likely to achieve positive outcomes from justice systems. Any disadvantage creates vulnerability and offenders target vulnerability.

Policing, like many other organisations in recent times, is coming to terms with the ubiquitous expressions of "victim-centric" and "trauma-informed," suggesting a greater focus on the needs of victims and developing responses that are more therapeutic. This marks a significant shift in language and practise, moving away from practises and attitudes that victims found unsatisfactory, or even abusive. Recent rises in reporting in many common law countries mark not only a shift in public attitudes, but also an acknowledgment that policing has made some progress in providing processes and practises more suited to the needs of those victimised by sexual and family violence perpetrators. It is important to note, however, that these changes are still in their infancy, and have barely begun in some jurisdictions.

Public attitudes too can be slow to shift, leaving many myths and misconceptions of both sexual and relationship crime to be challenged and eradicated. Policing has a long legacy of disbelieving victims of family and sexual violence, particularly women and children. A recent Australian survey, conducted by the national broadcaster, found that a mere 55% of respondents agreed with the statement, "Allegations of sexual assault are almost always true," despite decades of evidence that false reporting is low (Tidmarsh & Hamilton 2020). A previous survey, conducted only two years earlier attracted only 41% affirmative responses, suggesting there has been some change in ideas and attitudes (ABC 2019).

The reason these myths and misconceptions are important is that they frame our understanding of victim behaviour, influencing police, prosecutors, and the public who make up the "fact finders" in any trial. For example, victim behaviour in sexual offence cases has often been described as "counter-intuitive," usually marked as a criticism of no resistance or injury, or delay in complaint. The term lacks any understanding of the dynamics of sexual offending relationships, but it denotes both the enduring strength of some misconceptions, and how hard it is for us to provide genuinely "victim-centric" responses while so many persist.

Whilst there are differences between myths and misconceptions of sexual offending and family violence, there are many similarities, particularly those centred on the "counter-intuitive" notion that victims would remain in continued relationship with offenders and would not report abuses when they occur. Importantly, most misconceptions concern victim behaviour, rather than offenders, suggesting scepticism about women and children's voices remains strong.

Here in Victoria, Australia, where we reside, we have challenged police culture and practise regarding sexual offending by focusing on offenders' behaviour first, emphasising the logic of victims' behaviour as a response to offenders' actions. This focus required a methodology that helped investigators understand the entirety of the abusive relationship, particularly the grooming behaviour that demanded victims respond as the perpetrator wanted, which led to the creation of the Whole Story investigation and interviewing methodology (Tidmarsh 2021). At the core of Whole Story is an understanding that offending begins with offenders, and that victim behaviour can only be understood once the entire relationship is explored. The first step in victim-centric policing is to listen to victims and explore the breadth and depth of their experience.

Trauma-informed approaches also demand a detailed understanding of victims' experience, including the impact on memory and mental health. Importantly, in understanding the impacts of trauma, institutions and organisations must be careful not to replicate the abusive power dynamics victims have experienced during abusive experiences and relationships. Each step of the disclosure, reporting, investigation, and prosecution processes must be thought through, to ensure that processes are therapeutic, as far as is possible, to maximise the elicitation of available evidence should forensic pathways be sought, and provide victims with the services and justice pathways they choose. Contrary to popular belief, victims often want a variety of responses, not just punishment, but alternative pathways are the exception rather than the rule in many countries. Often, in both sexual offending and family violence cases, victims just want the abuse to stop, and to live in safety. These wishes raise uncomfortable issues both for police and the wider public.

In terms of our responses to victims of sexual offending and family violence, we offer few choices, particularly responses to sexual offending. Victims are left with recourse to the service systems, for therapeutic and practical assistance, or to the adversarial system if they wish to seek a justice outcome. Adversarial processes focus on the state as the injured party, relegating victims to witnesses of their own story. They are often accused of replicating the abuses of power that victims have come to report. As we have seen, in analysing the behaviour of offenders, and their focus on silencing and controlling victims, it is a persuasive argument. Furthermore, victims' needs vary widely following the impacts of abusive behaviour on their unique personalities and circumstances. Their definitions of justice may also vary widely, with some preferring responses that do not come with the aggressive terminology of "adversarial" (Henry, Powell, & Flynn 2015). These ideas will be unpacked and explored further in subsequent chapters.

Methodology and chapter overview

Before embarking on research for this book, we received ethics approval from RMIT University and Victoria Police ethics committees in Australia. This book largely draws on international peer-reviewed literature from the last 40 years. The book is also informed by interviews with 12 Australian stakeholders (largely frontline practitioners) who have professional expertise in the fields of family violence and/or sexual offending. Stakeholders were asked about their professional role, their perceptions of the strengths and challenges of addressing family violence and sexual offending according to the same framework, as well as their thoughts on future policies and campaigns. They were encouraged to offer working examples where possible, but with no identifying details of any clients. Stakeholder quotes are interspersed throughout chapters of this book to illustrate key issues. Respective stakeholder names or pseudonyms are provided with permission. We also try to prioritise the voices of victim-survivors (from extant research and publicly available quotes) to humanise the issues of family violence and sexual offending.

Terminology regarding family violence, domestic abuse, and sexual offending will be discussed in Chapter 1. Chapter 1 will also examine the historical, cultural, and legal underpinnings of various definitions regarding "family violence," "sexual offending," and "intimate partner sexual violence." It will consider the assumptions and theories that underlie different conceptualisations, and how language has evolved over time. Understanding how family violence and sexual offending is defined—and what language is used—is integral to how policies and responses are operationalised.

Chapter 2 will reflect on the political landscapes that have shaped policies regarding family violence and sexual offending (predominantly in Australia, the United States, and the United Kingdom). It examines government funding attached to family violence and sexual offending and the effect this has on various services. It also explores the increased focus on family and sexual violence in recent years, drawing on Victoria's Royal Commission into Family Violence (2016) and Australia's National Plan to reduce violence against women and their children 2010–2022 to highlight implications of treating sexual offending according to a family violence framework.

Chapter 3 will explore public understandings of family violence and sexual offending, as well as common myths and misconceptions. Media representations, international surveys, awareness-raising, and prevention campaigns will be used to illustrate public understandings and build on the argument that the way we characterise family violence and sexual offending may have broader criminal justice consequences. For example, what are the implications on reporting rates when we frame family violence and sexual offending as separate and/or embedded constructs?

Chapter 4 will highlight how reports of family violence and sexual offending are policed, with a focus on how sexual offences are investigated when considered within and outside of intimate partner relationships. It uses de-identified case studies from Victoria Police to illustrate questions around police discretion, evidence-gathering, and prosecution. For example, which internal police department takes on a report of sexual assault when it occurs within an intimate partner relationship? What evidence do police focus on? Which offences are easier to prosecute? Implications will be discussed, along with a focus on the Whole Story approach to sexual assault investigations (Tidmarsh et al. 2012). Here, we concentrate on issues around grooming, coercive control, consent, counter-intuitive victim-survivor behaviour, and corroboration.

Chapter 5 is dedicated to child victims of sexual abuse. It will examine literature and statistics on the occurrence of child sexual abuse within families where domestic violence is present. It will also examine correlations between children's exposure to domestic violence and experiences of child sexual abuse. We draw on stakeholder interviews and case studies to argue that child abuse can get overlooked if the main focus is on traditional domestic violence between intimate partners. We also emphasise the importance of recognising children as victims of family violence, rather than as extensions of their parent's abuse or simply witnesses to an abusive event.

Chapter 6 will present comparative commentary on how we treat, punish, and respond to offenders of family and/or sexual violence. We focus on the various criminal justice and treatment options available to those who are charged with family violence and/or sexual offences (e.g., intervention orders, family violence safety notices, men's behavioural change programmes, sex offender treatment programmes). We also examine court processes, conviction and attrition rates of sexual offence cases compared to family violence cases. We deliberate whether perpetrators of family violence are treated more leniently than those considered to be sex offenders, and what this might mean for future policies and procedures.

The final chapter will conclude with key implications of current conceptualisations and frameworks for preventing and responding to family violence and sexual offending. It provides suggestions for future research and practise, with a focus on social service and criminal justice reforms. It ends with a critical but optimistic view of how we can maintain the two lenses, and ultimately strengthen our approaches to family violence and sexual offending.

References

ABC News, 2019. Australia talks: Data explorer. www.abc.net.au/news/2020-12-10/australia-talks-data-explorer-2019/12946988#/

Abel, G.G., Becker, J.V., Mittelman, M., Cunningham-Rathner, J., Rouleau, J.L., and Murphy, W.D., 1987. Self-reported sex crimes of nonincarcerated paraphiliacs. *Journal of Interpersonal Violence*, *2*(1), pp. 3–25. doi:10.1177/088626087002001001

ABS, 2017. *Personal safety, Australia, 2016.* ABS cat. no. 4906.0, Australian Bureau of Statistics, Canberra.

ABS, 2020. *Recorded crime – Victims, Australia.* Australian Bureau of Statistics, Canberra.

AIHW, 2021. *Family, domestic and sexual violence in Australia: Australia's welfare 2021.* Australian Institute of Health & Welfare, Canberra.

Appel, A.E. and Holden, G.W., 1998. The co-occurrence of spouse and physical child abuse: a review and appraisal. *Journal of Family Psychology*, *12*(4), pp. 578–599.

Bagwell-Gray, M.E., Messing, J.T., and Baldwin-White, A., 2015. Intimate partner sexual violence: A review of terms, definitions, and prevalence. *Trauma, Violence, & Abuse*, *16*(3), pp. 316–335. doi:10.1177/1524838014557290

Bard, L.A., Carter, D.L., Cerce, D.D., Knight, R.A., Rosenberg, R., and Schneider, B., 1987. A descriptive study of rapists and child molesters: Developmental, clinical, and criminal characteristics. *Behavioral Sciences & the Law*, *5*(2), pp. 203–220. doi:10.1002/bsl.2370050211

Becker, J.V., Harris, C.D., and Sales, B.D., 2013. Juveniles who commit sexual offenses: A critical review of research. In Hall, G. C. N., Hirschman, R., Graham, J. R., & Zaragoza, M. S. (Eds.), *Sexual Aggression*, pp. 235–248. Taylor & Francis, New York.

Bedi, G. and Goddard, C., 2007. Intimate partner violence: What are the impacts on children?. *Australian Psychologist*, *42*(1), pp. 66–77. doi:10.1080/00050060600726296

Beech, A.R., Parrett, N., Ward, T., and Fisher, D., 2009. Assessing female sexual offenders' motivations and cognitions: An exploratory study. *Psychology, Crime & Law*, *15*(2–3), pp. 201–216. doi:10.1080/10683160802190921

Bidarra, Z.S., Lessard, G., and Dumont, A., 2016. Co-occurrence of intimate partner violence and child sexual abuse: Prevalence, risk factors and related issues. *Child Abuse & Neglect*, *55*, pp. 10–21. doi:10.1016/j.chiabu.2016.03.007

Bowdler, M., 2020. *Is rape a crime?: A memoir, an investigation, and a manifesto*. Flatiron Books, New York.

Boxall, H., Morgan, A., and Brown, R., 2021. *Experiences of domestic violence among women with restrictive long-term health conditions* (No. AIC Statistical Report 32). Australian Institute of Criminology, Canberra.

Cortoni, F., Babchishin, K.M., and Rat, C., 2016. The proportion of sexual offenders who are female is higher than thought: A meta-analysis. *Criminal Justice and Behavior*, *44*(2), pp. 145–162. doi:10.1177/0093854816658923

Craissati, J. and Beech, A., 2004. The characteristics of a geographical sample of convicted rapists: Sexual victimization and compliance in comparison to child molesters. *Journal of Interpersonal Violence*, *19*(4), pp. 371–388. doi:10.1177/0886260503262078

Craven, S., Brown, S., and Gilchrist, E., 2006. Sexual grooming of children: Review of literature and theoretical considerations. *Journal of Sexual Aggression*, *12*(3), pp. 287–299. doi:10.1080/13552600601069414

Dhawan, S. and Marshall, W.L., 1996. Sexual abuse histories of sexual offenders. *Sexual Abuse*, *8*(1), pp. 7–15. doi:10.1177/107906329600800102

Donegan, M. 2020. *Should we stop calling rape victims 'survivors'*? The Guardian, 15 August.

Dorahy, M.J. and Clearwater, K., 2012. Shame and guilt in men exposed to childhood sexual abuse: A qualitative investigation. *Journal of Child Sexual Abuse*, *21*(2), pp. 155–175. 10.1080/10538712.2012.659803F

Femicide Census, 2021. *UK femicides 2009–2018*. London.

Gilchrist, E., 2009. Implicit thinking about implicit theories in intimate partner violence. *Psychology, Crime & Law*, *15*(2–3), pp. 131–145. doi:10.1080/10683160802190863

Hackett, S., 2014. *Children and young people with harmful sexual behaviours*. Research in Practice, Dartington, Devon.

Hamby, S., Finkelhor, D., Turner, H., and Ormrod, R., 2010. The overlap of witnessing partner violence with child maltreatment and other victimizations in a nationally representative survey of youth. *Child Abuse & Neglect*, *34*(10), pp. 734–741. doi:10.1016/j.chiabu.2010.03.001

Henry, N., Powell, A., and Flynn, A. eds., 2015. *Rape justice: Beyond the criminal law*. Springer, Hampshire.

Herrenkohl, T.I., Sousa, C., Tajima, E.A., Herrenkohl, R.C., and Moylan, C.A., 2008. Intersection of child abuse and children's exposure to domestic violence. *Trauma, Violence, & Abuse*, *9*(2), pp. 84–99. doi:10.1177/1524838008314797

Jespersen, A.F., Lalumière, M.L., and Seto, M.C., 2009. Sexual abuse history among adult sex offenders and non-sex offenders: A meta-analysis. *Child Abuse & Neglect*, *33*(3), pp. 179–192. doi:10.1016/j.chiabu.2008.07.004

Knight, R.A., 1999. Validation of a typology for rapists. *Journal of Interpersonal Violence*, *14*(3), pp. 303–330. doi:10.1177/088626099014003006

Maher, J. and McCulloch, J. 2020. *Shifting the visual story on women who have experienced domestic violence*. Monash University, Melbourne.

ONS, 2018. *Sexual offending: victimisation and the path through the criminal justice system*. Office for National Statistics, London.

RAINN, 2022. *How often does sexual assault occur in the United States?* Rape, Abuse & Incest National Network, Washington.

Ramirez, S.R., Jeglic, E.L., and Calkins, C., 2015. An examination of the relationship between childhood abuse, anger and violent behavior among a sample of sex offenders. *Health & Justice*, *3*(1), pp. 1–10. doi:10.1186/s40352-015-0025-3

Seghorn, T.K., Prentky, R.A., and Boucher, R.J., 1987. Childhood sexual abuse in the lives of sexually aggressive offenders. *Journal of the American Academy of Child & Adolescent Psychiatry*, *26*(2), pp. 262–267. Doi:10.1097/00004583-198703000-00025

Simons, D.A., Wurtele, S.K., and Durham, R.L., 2008. Developmental experiences of child sexual abusers and rapists. *Child Abuse & Neglect*, *32*(5), pp. 549–560. doi:10.1016/j.chiabu.2007.03.027

Stark, E., 2006. *Coercive control: How men entrap women in personal life.* Oxford University Press, New York.

Stemple, L., Flores, A., and Meyer, I.H., 2017. Sexual victimization perpetrated by women: Federal data reveal surprising prevalence. *Aggression and Violent Behavior*, *34*, pp. 302–311. doi:10.1016/j.avb.2016.09.007

Tarczon, C. and Quadara, A., 2012. *The nature and extent of sexual assault and abuse in Australia.* Australian Institute of Family Studies, Melbourne.

Tidmarsh, P., 2021. *The Whole Story: Investigating sexual crime–truth, lies and the path to justice.* Random House, Melbourne.

Tidmarsh, P. and Hamilton, G., 2020. Misconceptions of sexual crimes against adult victims: Barriers to justice. *Trends and Issues in Crime and Criminal Justice*, *611*, pp. 1–18.

Tidmarsh, P., Powell, M.B., and Darwinkel, E., 2012. Whole Story': A new framework for conducting investigative interviews about sexual assault. *Investigative Interviewing: Research and Practice*, *4*(2), pp. 33–45.

Turner, H.A., Finkelhor, D., and Ormrod, R., 2010. Poly-victimization in a national sample of children and youth. *American Journal of Preventive Medicine*, *38*(3), pp. 323–330. doi:10.1016/j.amepre.2009.11.012

Victorian Government, 2016. *Royal Commission into family violence* (No. 132). Victoria, Australia.

Weldon, S. and Gilchrist, E., 2012. Implicit theories in intimate partner violence offenders. *Journal of Family Violence*, *27*(8), pp. 761–772.

WHO, 2021. *Violence against women prevalence estimates, 2018.* World Health Organisation, Geneva.

1

HOW DO WE DEFINE FAMILY VIOLENCE AND SEXUAL OFFENDING?

Conceptualisations of family violence and sexual offending have evolved over time, with varying definitions and frameworks in different jurisdictions. This chapter examines historical, cultural, and legal terminologies regarding "family violence" and "sexual offending." It draws on Liz Kelly's (1987) continuum of sexual violence and the assumptions and theories that underlie different conceptualisations. Particular attention is paid to intimate partner sexual violence and the need for a distinct and uniform definition. Finally, discussion is focused on the points of agreement and disjuncture between the family violence and sexual assault sectors, with a light cast on the differences between coercive control and grooming.

The nomenclature of violence within relationships

There is no uniform term that demarcates violence and abuse that is experienced, largely by women from men. Across English-speaking countries, there are a multitude of terms: domestic violence/abuse, intimate partner violence, family violence, sexual violence/abuse, sexual assault, rape, dating violence, violence against women, gendered violence, battering, coercive control, and intimate terrorism. All terms carry different rationales and limitations.

Intimate partner violence appears to be the most common term used in the United States (Goodmark 2018). Such a term denotes the context of the violence without limiting the relationship to marriage (e.g., wife/spouse abuse, marital rape). In Australia, an even broader term, "family violence," is commonly used to include a range of biological, familial, and intimate personal relationships. A family member can include children, current or former intimate partners, or people who are potentially perceived as family members (e.g., disability carers, people living in the same residential facility). The term "family" is also intended to reflect the diversity of kin relationships in Aboriginal and Torres Strait Islander communities, recognising that

DOI: 10.4324/9781003051657-2

definitions of relatives within these communities are often broader than mainstream Western families (Victorian Government 2016).

Our interviews with professional stakeholders revealed conflicting views about the use of the term family violence. Some stakeholders thought that family violence was a culturally inclusive umbrella term that encapsulated various forms of violence beyond a husband and wife or nuclear family:

> I call it family violence because I think it captures all of it, even if the offending is from an uncle to a child or something like that, I think it captures all the offending within that family context—it's not necessarily biological.
>
> *Rebecca: counsellor and advocate at a sexual violence service*

Other advocates at family and sexual violence services felt that family violence was "sanitised" language and a "watered down version of what's actually happening." They instead suggested the use of more explicit terms such as "child sexual abuse" and "dating violence" so that distinct issues do not lose attention or meaning.

In the United Kingdom, there has been a gradual move to use the term *domestic abuse* in addition to domestic violence as a way of acknowledging both the physical and non-physical dimensions of abuse. After stakeholder consultations, the government in England and Wales amended their definition of domestic violence to include coercive control (Home Office 2012). This led to their current definition of domestic violence and abuse:

> Any incident or pattern of incidents of controlling, coercive or threatening behaviour, violence or abuse between those aged 16 or over who are or have been intimate partners or family members regardless of gender or sexuality. This can encompass but is not limited to the following types of abuse:
>
> - Psychological
> - Physical
> - Sexual
> - Financial
> - Emotional
> - Controlling behaviour

Controlling behaviours are various acts that have the intention of making a person dependent or subordinate. For example, a person who perpetrates domestic abuse may isolate their victim from family and friends, monitor and regulate their everyday activities, and deprive them of finances and resources needed to make free and independent decisions (Strickland & Allen 2018). Coercive behaviour is considered to be an act or pattern of acts designed to harm, punish, or frighten a victim (e.g., threats, assaults, humiliation, intimidation). In 2015, England and Wales became the first jurisdictions in the world to enshrine coercive controlling behaviours in criminal legislation, and we are seeing other nations, such as France and the United States, follow in their footsteps by adopting or considering similar actions.

The term domestic abuse has both strengths and shortcomings. On the one hand, it emphasises that domestic violence is rarely a single incident or form of violence, but rather a mixture and extended pattern of behaviours. It also helps to move the focus from physical violence to broader patterns of manipulation and power, and behaviours which are not considered to be inherently violent (Wright & Hearn 2013). In her book, "see what you made me do," investigative journalist, Jess Hill, contends that physical violence is rare in some of the worst abusive relationships; many women are abused in ways that are more subtle but just as damaging and potent. She writes: "as long as we conceal domestic abuse under umbrella terms like rape and assault, we will never fathom its true, visceral horror" (p. 347).

While domestic abuse captures the broader essence of victim-survivor's experiences, the terms *domestic* and *family* have been critiqued for their focus on the home, suggesting that this is a private problem between people who share a household (Wright & Hearn 2013). Dr. Rachael Burgin, Executive Director of Rape and Sexual Assault Research and Advocacy, explained in one of our interviews, "when we use a word like family violence, we forget that it is not captured in the walls of a family home—it festers in every corner of people's lives." Terms such as domestic and family violence/abuse and intimate partner violence also fail to encapsulate the gendered nature of the problem. It is an unequivocal finding that most people who perpetrate domestic violence are male, and the majority of people subjected to abuse are female (ABS 2017; Hester 2009; ONS 2019). Using gender-neutral language may minimise the role that gender plays in domestic violence and compromise our ability to address core factors in policy, prevention, and response efforts. Yet, using gendered language also poses its own issues. Sharon Simon, Industry Fellow in family violence, explained further in one of our interviews:

> Every label is difficult, every label I find challenging. In my [previous role] I was very gendered in my language (e.g., violence against women), but what does that mean for LGBTQIA+ the community? Family violence de-genders so much, it provides so many uses and is more inclusive, but also so many disadvantages in terms of losing our gendered understanding of violence. How can we use gendered language and be inclusive of the LGBTQIA+ community?

It is clear there is no perfect universal term to describe violence that occurs between family members and intimate partners. Recent policies and legislation appear to adopt multiple terms (e.g., domestic and family violence; or domestic violence and abuse) to try to accurately reflect the different dynamics of the problem. Regardless of what terms are used, it is important for legislators and policymakers to consciously reflect on the language they use and consider the implications for their local stakeholders and service users. Providing rationales for underlying positions will also be helpful in understanding what is meant by certain terminology.

In the current book, we are inclined to use terms "domestic and family violence" where appropriate. As both authors are Australian, we have decided to use family violence in line with the preferences of many Aboriginal and Torres Strait Islander communities (Mitchell 2011). The broader term also better reflects the topics included in this book, as Chapter 5 will consider how the focus on intimate partner violence may neglect children as victims of domestic violence and sexual abuse. Thus, our definition is the same as domestic abuse above, but also includes, "behaviour by a person that causes a child to hear or witness, or otherwise be exposed to the effects of [domestic abuse]" (Family Violence Protection Act 2008 Vic).

It should also be clear that we adopt a feminist understanding of family violence, whereby we view broader patriarchal social structures and unequal gendered power relations as being key to men's and women's experiences of violence. We also acknowledge that people's experiences of violence are impacted by different forms of systematic disadvantage based on intersecting characteristics such as race, sexuality, disability, and socio-economic status (Crenshaw 1991). As such, our underlying lens is as odds with alternate theories such as conflict theories, which assume that violence and aggression are normal ways of diffusing conflict in interpersonal relationships, and that couples are mutually responsible for violent incidents, regardless of their gender or position of power (Cox 2015).

Definitions of sexual violence over time and place

Broadly speaking, sexual violence can be defined as any act (or attempted act) of a sexual nature perpetrated by one person against another without the victim's consent (WHO 2002). But as with domestic and family violence, there is a lack of consensus regarding terminology around sexual violence. Firstly, a distinction can be made between offence-based and experience-based definitions. Offence-based definitions recognise sexual acts that are deemed illegal (e.g., rape, sexual assault, indecent assault). Experience-based definitions are more victim-survivor centred and tend to recognise a broader range of sexually harmful or abusive behaviours that are not necessarily proscribed in law (ABS 2004; Victorian Government 2016). An example of an experience-based definition of sexual assault is as follows.

Sexual assault is unwanted behaviour of a sexual nature directed towards a person:

- Which makes that person feel uncomfortable, distressed, frightened, or threatened, or which results in harm or injury to that person.
- To which that person has not freely agreed or given consent, or to which that person is not capable of giving consent.
- In which another person uses physical, emotional, psychological, or verbal force or (other) coercive behaviour against that person (ABS 2004).

Liz Kelly was one of the first researchers to adopt experience-based definitions of sexual violence by allowing women to describe their experiences in their own words. Based on interviews with 60 women, Kelly demonstrated how women's experiences of sexual violence seldom fit neatly into existing legal categories; rather, they were more likely to blur into one another, with women's understandings of their experiences sometimes changing over time (Kelly 1988). This led Kelly to develop the "continuum of sexual violence," which ranges from everyday encounters of sexism through to the murder of women and girls. Such a framework allows for new terms and definitions to evolve (e.g., coercive and pressurised sex) and helps women to recognise experiences as abusive in the absence of fitting legal terminology (Kelly 1988).

Language is clearly an important mechanism for victim-survivors to name, and, in turn, validate their experiences. Kelly (1988) has argued that it is in perpetrators' best interests to narrow the definitions of sexual violence as it limits their chances of being held accountable for abusive behaviour: "At the same time as women are unable to name their abuse as abuse, men are able to deny responsibility for abusive behaviour. Language is a further means of controlling women" (p. 156). This notion is supported by data sources that indicate lower rates of sexual violence when narrower offence-based definitions are used (ABS 2004). Likewise, scholars Wright and Hearn (2013) have emphasised that narrow definitions of violence which concentrate on individual people or incidents neglect the broader structures that produce or enable violence to continue. They contend that "violence and violation need to be seen in an open-ended way…they need to be linked with other negative processes, such as oppression, exploitation, and marginalization" (p. 38).

A second point of contention surrounding definitions of sexual violence is whether behaviours are considered sexual or physical in nature. Feminist writer and activist, Susan Brownmiller, asserted that rape is about the exertion of male power and control rather than sexual gratification (Brownmiller 1975). Indeed, campaigners have suggested that defining rape as a physically violent rather than a sexual crime could benefit victim-survivors in the criminal justice system by removing the consent defence and avoiding a focus on victim's sexual histories (Kelly 1988). Yet, others have argued that sexual violence has unique sexual features, over and above physical violence, that cannot be overlooked. For example, recent interviews with 38 victim-survivors of intimate partner sexual violence suggested that sexual elements were core to survivor's understandings of their experiences and created unique hurdles for recovery (Tarzia 2020). Many interviewees vocalised that they wished physical abuse was "all that had happened," and that their experiences were *sexually* de-humanising, resulting in a "different kind of damage" to physical or psychological abuse (p. 5). Kelly (1988) reconciled that the varied experiences of rape make it impossible to categorise rape as physical *or* sexual, as each incident will involve both aspects—albeit to varying degrees.

As with the terms domestic and family violence, a further area of debate is around the term sexual *violence.* On the one hand, the term sexual violence captures the full range of sexually harmful behaviours without having to define specific categories or offences (e.g., sexual harassment, rape, child sexual abuse). Kelly (1988) also highlighted that sexual violence can be considered "violent" even in the absence of physical violence because there are behaviours that signal the threat of violence (e.g., clenching a fist, destroying furniture or possessions). Many women in her research reported submitting to their partner's demands for sex because of a fear of further physical violence. More recently, victim-survivor and advocate, Geraldine Bilston (2020), described how the abuse she experienced from her ex-partner was violent, even in the absence of physical violence:

> I remember a time after a particularly brutal onslaught of verbal abuse where I sat on the floor crying, absolutely beaten by his words.
>
> I told him: "I don't want to be here anymore, I just can't go on."
>
> He responded… by laughing. I may not have had a bruise or any broken bones that day, but I was seriously injured. This was violence and I was not safe at home.

On the other hand, there is concern that using the term "violence" may help to perpetuate the rape myth that "real rape" involves being violently attacked and injured by a stranger. This is contrary to the research evidence which indicates that sexual offending is a profoundly relationship-based crime, whereby offenders are often known by their victim (AIHW 2018; Department of Justice 2017; Tidmarsh & Hamilton 2020). Offenders frequently engage in a "grooming" process where they exploit power and trust to gradually manipulate their victim into compliance, without the need for weapons or physical violence. Indeed, studies have shown that many victim-survivors did not sustain physical injuries during a rape (Carr et al. 2014; Waterhouse, Reynolds, & Egan 2016). Moreover, physical violence may not be present during a rape because victim-survivors may freeze or cooperate rather than physically resist the offender. This freezing reaction is also known as involuntary paralysis or "tonic immobility" (Heidt, Marx, & Forsyth 2005; Kalaf et al. 2017). The key concern here is that victim-survivors may not recognise their experiences as "sexual violence" if traditional physical violence has not been present.

In the current book, we have decided to largely use the term "sexual offending." The reasons for this are manifold. Firstly, we believe that "offending" better represents the acts and/or abuses in question. It focuses on the behaviour of perpetrators and signals that an active process was involved (i.e., the offender engaged in tactics to manipulate, control, and abuse their victim—violently, or otherwise). The term makes it clear that the victim-survivor is not responsible for what they have been subjected to. "Sexual offending" also encapsulates the types of behaviours used by perpetrators in one-off rapes and sexual assaults through to more long-term abuses, often by intimate partners and family members. The term is, of course, not perfect. As discussed above, not all sexual harms are technically "offences," and the term frames sexual offending as a criminal justice problem as opposed to a health or social issue. Nevertheless, the current book adopts a largely criminological lens around sexual offending and family violence and explores their intersections often in relation to policing and criminal justice contexts. Therefore, we conclude it is the most appropriate term for the topics covered in this book, and we also encourage policymakers and stakeholders to consider its use.

While we mostly use the term sexual offending, offence-based terms such as rape, sexual assault, and sexual abuse will also arise where appropriate. It is important to explain these terms, especially since there are varying meanings across jurisdictions (even within countries), and there have been significant changes to legal terminologies in recent decades. For instance, it was only in 2012 that the United States' FBI expanded their definition of rape to include: "the penetration, no matter how slight, of the vagina or anus with any body part or object, or oral penetration by a sex organ of another person, without the consent of the victim" (Department of Justice 2012). Previously, the definition only recognised forcible male penile penetration of a female vagina. Other Western countries such as Australia have adopted similar definitions, although rape in England, Wales, and Scotland is still limited to penile penetration.

Some countries, such as Canada and New Zealand (and some states within Australia), include rape as a form sexual assault. Sexual assault is commonly recognised as, "any unwanted forced sex act or behaviour that has happened without a person's consent" (New Zealand Police 2020). This can include a broader range of behaviours such as unwanted sexual touching, kissing, exposure of genitals, and forcing the victim-survivor to touch the offender in a sexual way. Sexual abuse is largely used to describe sexual acts of maltreatment towards children. It recognises that children are incapable of providing informed consent to any sex act. The age of consent varies in different countries, but typically sits around 16 to 18 years in Western countries.

To further complicate legal understandings of rape and sexual assault, there is a lack of consensus regarding definitions of *consent*, between and even within countries. As Australian of the year 2021, Grace Tame, highlighted in her National Press Club address, "we have eight different state and territory jurisdictions and eight different definitions of consent." While consent is generally understood as free and voluntary agreement, where the person has capacity to make a choice about sexual activity, some jurisdictions have the requirement that consent must be positively communicated, either by words and/or conduct (e.g., Victoria, *Crimes Act 1958*). This is often referred to as an affirmative consent model. Other jurisdictions, however, have no such requirement (e.g., Western Australia), meaning an accused does not necessarily have to show they took any steps to ascertain whether the complainant was consenting. Seemingly small and nuanced differences in language and definitions can have considerable impacts on sexual offence cases and convictions, emphasising the importance of examining legal definitions in depth and moving towards more consistent definitions for clearer public understandings.

Language surrounding sexual offences also signals important messages about how we view and respond to such crimes. This point was emphasised again by activist and advocate for survivors of sexual assault, Grace Tame, in her 2021 National Press Club speech:

> Let's start by considering the implications of linguistics related to offences. Through #LetHerSpeak campaign efforts, we saw the wording of my abuser's

> charge officially changed from maintaining a sexual relationship to a person under 17, to the persistent sexual abuse of a child. Think about the difference in the crime according to the language of both of these. Think about the message it sends to the community. Think about the message it sends survivors. Where empathy is placed, where blame is placed, and how punishment is then given.

We must consider these broader insinuations when devising and revising definitions of both family violence and sexual offending, particularly in legal settings. Language that indirectly minimises or maximises the seriousness of crimes and behaviours within the media will be explored further in Chapter 3.

Intimate partner sexual violence

Intimate partner sexual violence (IPSV) is a clear way in which family violence and sexual offending intersect, yet it is often poorly understood and lacks a uniform definition. Indeed, a review of U.S. literature on sexual violence in intimate relationships found 14 different terms defined in 29 different ways to describe IPSV (Bagwell-Gray et al. 2015). The varying and at times conflicting definitions, may be due to a range of factors. Firstly, IPSV is a relatively recent criminal offence. In the United States, for example, marital rape was not outlawed in all 50 states until 1993 (Bennice & Resick 2003; Bagwell-Gray et al. 2015). In some countries, such as India, rape within marriage is still not considered a criminal act. In the Talking Research podcast (2020), Dr. Sreeparna Chattopadhyay discusses how marital rape in India is common but difficult to accurately measure because it is a taboo subject. She remarks that consent within a relationship is often assumed and marital rape is not viewed as a serious issue.

Secondly, varied definitions of IPSV may exist because sexual violence is a sensitive topic that is difficult to measure. Victim-survivors and perpetrators may not recognise behaviours or experiences as rape or sexual assault. Victim-survivors may be sexually inexperienced upon entering a relationship with their abusive partner and lack a frame of reference for what is considered consensual and healthy sexual behaviour (Tarzia 2020). Victim-survivors of IPSV have reported that sex often started as consensual, but gradually became more coerced over time (Kelly 1988). Victim-survivors may also minimise the sexual component of abuse as a coping mechanism and be reluctant to label a loved partner as a "rapist" (Kelly 1998; McOrmond-Plummer 2009). This may, in part, be due to the enduring rape myth that real rape only occurs between strangers in a dark alleyway. For example, one in three Australians are unaware that a woman is more likely to be sexually assaulted by a known person rather than a stranger, and 19% are unaware that non-consensual sex in marriage is illegal (Webster et al. 2018).

Inconsistent definitions of IPSV may also be due to varying legal definitions across jurisdictions, as well as different terms between disciplines (Bagwell-Gray et al. 2015). Bagwell-Gray and colleagues emphasise the need for a shared definition of

IPSV in order to more accurately measure its prevalence, effects, and consequences, and to effectively guide intervention and prevention measures. They have in turn proposed the use of a quadrant taxonomy of IPSV that takes into account penetrative and non-penetrative acts, as well as the use of physical and non-physical force. This taxonomy condenses the previous array of definitions but still recognises the broad spectrum of victim-survivor's experiences (Bagwell-Gray 2019, p. 8):

- Intimate partner sexual coercion: the use of non-physical, controlling, degrading, and manipulative tactics to obtain, or attempt to obtain, unwanted oral, vaginal, or anal intercourse, including forced penetration and sex with objects.
- Intimate partner sexual assault: the use of physical violence or the threat of physical violence to obtain or attempt to obtain unwanted oral, vaginal, or anal intercourse, including forced penetration and sex with objects. Also includes unwanted penetration when a victim/survivor is unable to consent or is "unaware," i.e., asleep or under the influence of drugs and alcohol.
- Intimate partner sexual abuse: the use of manipulative, psychologically abusive tactics to keep an intimate partner in submissive positions of power; strategies include sexual degradation, non-contact unwanted sexual experiences, and reproductive and sexual control.
- Physically forced sexual activity: unwanted sexual experiences involving touch but not sexual penetration, such as being kissed in a sexual way, or having sexual body parts fondled or grabbed.

A distinct and unified definition of IPSV is important, particularly for victim-survivors. McOrmond-Plummer (2009) has highlighted that IPSV does not always fit neatly into the extant categories of domestic violence or sexual violence outside of relationships. If considered simply as rape, victim-survivors may not feel that their experiences are legitimate and may find it difficult to receive tailored and specialised services to promote effective recovery. She reflects on her own experiences as a member in a generic rape survivor support group:

> It was as if there was a hole in the knowledge; my experiences had only limited commonality. It left me feeling as if what happened to me was given lip-service as rape, but somehow "less" rape than any other kind. I believed that my level of trauma must be an overreaction, and was embarrassed about putting it on a par with the rapes of other women.
>
> *p. 8*

Conversely, it may be inadequate to conceive IPSV as just another form of domestic violence. While IPSV often happens in conjunction with other forms of abuse (e.g., physical, psychological, financial), victim-survivors who experience rape and/or coerced sex in the absence of other abuses may not identify their experience as domestic violence (McOrmond-Plummer 2009). Moreover, victim-survivor accounts suggest that IPSV is one of the worst types of abuse, and yet it often goes unreported and is rarely the focus of enquiries by domestic violence services (Tarzia 2020). As one victim-survivor recounted, "When people talk about physical assaults and financial and emotional, that's fine. Legitimately I'm a victim in all of those things. When you start talking about sexual things everybody is very, very uncomfortable" (Tarzia 2020). This notion is paralleled in one of our interviews with Sarah Hill, a counsellor advocate at a co-located family violence and sexual assault centre:

> We are trained to ask that question [whether the victim-survivor experienced sexual assault] and I think that's one of the things that concerns me about the sector is that it's an uncomfortable conversation for everybody to have, we know that, but if we don't ask we don't find out, so we always try and talk to our newer workers coming in about that, giving them the confidence to have those conversations—if you don't explore that you'll never find out what's happened, and quite often it leads to the victims needing support around those issues, whether its practical support around accessing medical care or counselling, or just knowing what their rights are around being a victim-survivor of sexual assault.

The above quotes, from both the victim-survivor and family violence worker perspectives, highlight the importance of treating IPSV as a core experience of family violence rather than an incidental issue. They also demonstrate how the strong taboo of sexual assault can make it incredibly difficult to uncover, but if a victim-survivor is referred or seeks help through a family violence agency, the onus rests on family violence workers to initiate those conversations about sexual violence, rather than only focusing on non-sexual physical violence. As Bergen (1996) raised over 25 years ago, "when treated as battered women, the wounds left by the sexual abuse often go unaddressed" (p. 11).

In sum, IPSV straddles both the sexual assault and family violence sectors, and warrants recognition in its own right. According to McOrmond-Plummer (2009), IPSV is best described as a "both/and" issue rather than an "either/or," with its own distinct features. It is clearly important that both sectors have an understanding about IPSV as a victim-survivor's unique needs may not be met if their abuse is only viewed through one lens and addressed according to separate frameworks. Having a clear and uniform definition is one way of acknowledging and prioritising IPSV.

Grooming and coercive control: Different languages for different sectors

As raised in the introduction chapter, there are often different language preferences between the family violence and sexual offending sectors. For instance, "coercive control" appears to be the phrase of choice for workers in the family violence sphere, whereas, "grooming" is more commonly used amongst those working in the area of sexual offending. Yet both terms are denoting very similar behaviours. To reiterate, coercive control typically refers to a pattern of tactics used to harm, intimidate, and exert power over another person in a relationship (Stark 2006). Examples of tactics include threats, isolating the victim from others, monitoring their everyday activities, and making them dependent on the perpetrator. The phrase is used largely in reference to adults. Grooming, on the other hand, is used primarily with children. It typically refers to how the offender manipulates the victim, their surrounding environment, and the victim's significant others to establish trust, power, and control, before moving to a sexual stage where they gradually sexualise the relationship, often beginning with non-threatening touches (e.g., hugging, tickling), followed by sexual abuse (Craven et al. 2006; Tidmarsh et al. 2012).

Coercive control and grooming are similar in several ways. They both describe a pattern of behaviours rather than discrete incidents, perpetrated largely by men. They both involve an active process of targeting and subjugating victims, while manipulating people and environments in order to minimise the chance of detection. Both concepts appeared to gain more formal recognition in the decade spanning 2000 to 2010, although legislation to criminalise grooming behaviours pre-dates that of coercive control. Moreover, victim-survivors of child sexual abuse are more vulnerable to becoming victims of family violence in adulthood, suggesting a clear link between victimisation of grooming and coercive control (Cox 2015; Garcia-Linares et al. 2005; Pico-Alfonso et al. 2006).

So why are different terms used and is there a need for different terms? We are beginning to recognise that adults can be the victims of sexually grooming behaviours too (Sinnamon 2017; Tidmarsh et al. 2012). Rebecca, a counsellor advocate, reported to us that she is seeing an increase in sexual assaults where adult victims have been groomed over dating apps such as Tinder and Bumble. Claire, a victim-survivor and campaigner against adult grooming, describes how her abuser researched her online and then falsely mirrored aspects of her life in order to create the illusion that they were soul mates: "He broke through my defences, built trust, and kept me in a relationship that defiled my values without me ever knowing until it was too late" (see CAAGe: the campaign against adult grooming). Yet the stigma attached to grooming may make victim-survivors and stakeholders reluctant to use the term with adults, particularly if the term is associated with something that happens to children: "as an adult you feel ashamed that you've been susceptible to being groomed" says Rebecca. Claire also echoes a similar point: "victims often feel shame, remorse and disgust at their participation. I'm no different. I felt filthy when I found out." Despite knowledge that grooming occurs with adults, legislation in many jurisdictions only recognises grooming with children. For example, in the United Kingdom, Australia, and New Zealand the offence of grooming applies to children under the age of 16, and under the age of 18 in the United States.

The difference between grooming and coercive control perhaps lies with their end goals. Sexual offending appears to be at the forefront of our understanding of grooming; abusers are often "priming" their victims to be sexually abused, although other motives might include financial exploitation, power, or trafficking

(Sinnamon 2017). Conversely, the end goal of coercive control is often the domination of another human, with sexual offending being one of the many tactics in achieving this goal. Based on the above research regarding intimate partner sexual violence, however, we contend that sexual offending warrants greater prominence in our collective conversations and understandings of coercive control. One of our interviewees, Narelle Goodland, reflects on her work as a principal practitioner at a policing organisation; she highlights how coercive control and grooming can be deeply intertwined in family violence situations:

> I like to always ask people in consultation, is that grooming or is that coercive control? Because the coercion and control or the violence is so visible that we could say yes that's coercion and control and that's about controlling mum, but how do we know it's not about sending a message to the daughter—that if you don't come tonight when I ask you to, you're being coerced into this sexual violent situation. How do we know that the violence towards mum, yes that's horrible for mum, but she might not be the primary victim; the primary victim might be the child. She's not at risk of death the mum, but the daughter is at risk of sexual abuse because our risk assessments are focused on harm in relation to [intimate partner violence], but sometimes it's not that at all.

This above quote demonstrates the complex relationship between coercive control and grooming. Violence and coercive control may be perpetrated against a partner, but it may be a means to an end, with sexual abuse of another family member (especially a child) as the ultimate aim. Family violence cases involving sexual abuse emphasise the requirement of varied practitioner awareness and knowledge about both coercive control and grooming behaviours. If practitioners examine cases solely through a family violence lens, they may interpret behaviour as coercive control and overlook important information about grooming and sexual abuse. Likewise, an approach that only focuses on grooming may miss broader patterns of coercive control. As Narelle Goodland summarised: "its so complex, if we're only looking at one component of it, we could be missing a whole other part of the story with that family that can keep on going." She also explained that a key part of her job is to prompt police to think about cases through a different lens, which helps to refresh ideas for different lines of inquiry and ultimately improve investigations—particularly in cases that were coming to a dead end. It would be wise for future research to further examine the parallels between grooming and coercive control, particularly from the perspectives of victim-survivors, perpetrators, and practitioners. Such research could have important implications for how we legislate against abusive behaviours and would be especially timely as countries implement and debate the criminalisation of coercive control.

Conclusion

This chapter explored the intersections of family violence and sexual offending at the definitional level. It exhibited the evolving definitions of family violence, sexual offending, and intimate partner sexual violence across both time and place. We have seen significant changes in how these concepts are defined in research, law, policy, and practise, and we continue to see further considerations, revisions, and refinements. In particular, it was evident that different sectors at times may adopt their own framework or lens for interpreting and responding to family violence and/or sexual offending (e.g., investigating behaviours as coercive control versus grooming; providing domestic violence services that overlook sexual abuse; offering rape support groups that do not cater to the needs of victim-survivors of intimate partner sexual violence). It is clear that language and definitions are not inconsequential: different conceptualisations may have important implications for a multitude of stakeholders (e.g., victim-survivors, perpetrators, policymakers, and practitioners). While specialist frameworks are undoubtedly important, the information in this chapter points to the need for more shared definitions and language amongst sectors and jurisdictions if we are to strengthen our responses to family violence and sexual offending.

References

ABS, 2004. *Sexual assault in Australia: A statistical overview*. cat. no. 4523.0. Australian Bureau of Statistics, Canberra.

ABS, 2017. *Personal safety, Australia, 2016*. ABS cat. no. 4906.0. Australian Bureau of Statistics, Canberra.

AIHW, 2018. *Family, domestic and sexual violence in Australia*. Australian Institute of Health & Welfare, Canberra.

Bagwell-Gray, M.E., 2019. Women's experiences of sexual violence in intimate relationships: Applying a new taxonomy. *Journal of Interpersonal Violence*, *36*(13–14), pp. 7813–7839. doi: 10.1177/0886260519827667

Bagwell-Gray, M.E., Messing, J.T., and Baldwin-White, A., 2015. Intimate partner sexual violence: A review of terms, definitions, and prevalence. *Trauma, Violence, & Abuse*, *16*(3), pp. 316–335. doi:10.1177/1524838014557290

Bennice, J.A. and Resick, P.A., 2003. Marital rape: History, research, and practice. *Trauma, Violence, & Abuse*, *4*(3), pp. 228–246. doi:10.1177/1524838003004003003

Bergen, R.K., 1996. *Wife rape* (Vol. 2). Sage, Thousand Oaks.

Bilston, G., 2020. *When I left my violent partner, my mum said my bruised face was a blessing*. Mamamia, Sydney.

Brownmiller, S., 1975. *Against our will: Men, women, and rape*. Fawcett Book, New York.

Carr, M., Thomas, A.J., Atwood, D., Muhar, A., Jarvis, K., and Wewerka, S.S., 2014. Debunking three rape myths. *Journal of Forensic Nursing*, *10*(4), pp. 217–225. doi:10.1097/JFN.0000000000000044

Cox, P., 2015. *Sexual assault and domestic violence in the context of co-occurrence and re-victimisation State of knowledge*. ANROWS, Sydney.

Craven, S., Brown, S., and Gilchrist, E., 2006. Sexual grooming of children: Review of literature and theoretical considerations. *Journal of Sexual Aggression, 12*(3), pp. 287–299. doi:10.1080/13552600601069414

Crenshaw, K., 1991. Mapping the margins: Identity politics, intersectionality, and violence against women. *Stanford Law Review, 43*(6), pp. 1241–1299.

Department of Justice, 2012. *An updated definition of rape*. The United States Department of Justice Archives, Washington.

Department of Justice, 2017. *National crime victimization survey, 2010–2016*. Office of Justice Programs, Bureau of Justice Statistics, Washington.

Family Violence Protection Act 2008 (Vic) (Austl.).

Garcia-Linares, M.I., Pico-Alfonso, M.A., Sanchez-Lorente, S., Savall-Rodriguez, F., Celda-Navarro, N., Blasco-Ros, C., and Martinez, M., 2005. Assessing physical, sexual, and psychological violence perpetrated by intimate male partners toward women: A Spanish cross-sectional study. *Violence and Victims, 20*(1), pp. 99–123. doi:10.1891/vivi.2005.20.1.99

Goodmark, L., 2018. *Decriminalizing domestic violence*. University of California Press, Berkeley.

Heidt, J.M., Marx, B.P., and Forsyth, J.P., 2005. Tonic immobility and childhood sexual abuse: A preliminary report evaluating the sequela of rape-induced paralysis. *Behaviour Research and Therapy, 43*(9), pp. 1157–1171. doi: 10.1016/j.brat.2004.08.005

Hester, M., 2009. *Who does what to whom?: Gender and domestic violence perpetrators*. University of Bristol [in association with] Northern Rock Foundation, Bristol.

Hill, J., 2019. *See what you made me do*. Black Inc, Carlton

Home Office, 2012. *New definition of domestic violence*. London.

Kalaf, J., Coutinho, E.S.F., Vilete, L.M.P., Luz, M.P., Berger, W., Mendlowicz, M., Volchan, E., Andreoli, S.B., Quintana, M.I., de Jesus Mari, J., and Figueira, I., 2017. Sexual trauma is more strongly associated with tonic immobility than other types of trauma: A population based study. *Journal of Affective Disorders, 215*, pp. 71–76. doi:10.1016/j.jad.2017.03.009

Kelly, L., 1988. *Surviving sexual violence*. John Wiley & Sons, Cambridge.

McOrmond-Plummer, L., 2009. *Considering the differences: Intimate partner sexual violence in sexual assault and domestic violence discourse*. IPSV, Washington Coalition of Sexual Assault Programs.

Mitchell, L., 2011. *Domestic violence in Australia: An overview of the issues*. Parliament of Australia, Canberra.

New Zealand Police, 2020. *Understanding sexual assault and consent*. New Zealand Government, Wellington.

ONS, 2019. *Domestic abuse prevalence and trends, England and Wales*. Office for National Statistics, London.

Pico-Alfonso, M.A., Garcia-Linares, M.I., Celda-Navarro, N., Blasco-Ros, C., Echeburúa, E., and Martinez, M., 2006. The impact of physical, psychological, and sexual intimate male partner violence on women's mental health: Depressive symptoms, posttraumatic stress disorder, state anxiety, and suicide. *Journal of Women's Health, 15*(5), pp. 599–611. doi:10.1089/jwh.2006.15.599

Sinnamon, G., 2017. The psychology of adult sexual grooming: Sinnamon's seven-stage model of adult sexual grooming. In W. Petherick, & G. Sinnamon (Eds.), *The psychology of criminal and antisocial behavior* (pp. 459–487). Academic Press, Amsterdam. doi:10.1016/B978-0-12-809287-3.00016-X

Stark, E., 2006. *Coercive control: How men entrap women in personal life*. Oxford University Press, New York.

Strickland, A. and Allen, G., 2018. *Domestic violence in England and Wales*. No. 6337, UK Parliament.

Tarzia, L., 2020. "It went to the very heart of who I was as a woman": The invisible impacts of intimate partner sexual violence. *Qualitative Health Research, 31*(2), pp. 287–297. doi:10.1177/1049732320967659

Tidmarsh, P. and Hamilton, G., 2020. Misconceptions of sexual crimes against adult victims: Barriers to justice. *Trends and Issues in Crime and Criminal Justice, 611*, pp. 1–18.

Tidmarsh, P., Powell, M.B., and Darwinkel, E., 2012. Whole story: A new framework for conducting investigative interviews about sexual assault. *Investigative Interviewing: Research and Practice*, *4*(2), pp. 33–45.

Victorian Government, 2016. *Royal Commission into family violence* (No. 132). Victoria.

Waterhouse, G.F., Reynolds, A., and Egan, V., 2016. Myths and legends: The reality of rape offences reported to a UK police force. *The European Journal of Psychology Applied to Legal Context, 8*(1), pp. 1–10. doi:10.1016/j.ejpal.2015.04.001

Webster, K., Diemer, K., Honey, N., Mannix, S., Mickle, J., Morgan, J., Parkes, A., Politoff, V., Powell, A., Stubbs, J. and Ward, A., 2018. *2017 National Community Attitudes towards Violence against Women Survey (NCAS): methodology report*. Australia's National Research Organisation for Women's Safety (ANROWS), Sydney.

WHO, 2002. *World report on violence and health*. World Health Organisation, Geneva.

Wright, C. and Hearn, J., 2013. Neutralizing gendered violence. In R. Klein (Ed.), *Framing sexual and domestic violence through language* (pp. 21–40). Palgrave Macmillan, New York.

2

POLICY CONTEXTS

When politics and funding dictate our approach to violence

The last decade has seen unprecedented attention to family violence and sexual offending, in what seems like a global awakening to issues that overwhelmingly impact women and children. The continued efforts of feminist activists, along with a series of high-profile tragedies have made it impossible for governments to ignore any longer. In 2013, the Justice Verma Commission was established in India following the fatal gang rape of a 23-year-old woman (commonly referred to by pseudonym, Nirbhaya) on a Delhi bus which garnered widespread national and international outrage. At the beginning of 2017, we saw millions of women and men donning pink "pussyhats" during the Women's March, one of the largest single-day protests in U.S. history, to denounce sexism and promote women's rights. The year ended with the a surge of sexual violence allegations online, widely known as the #metoo movement (True 2021).

More recently, we have seen governments across the world updating their plans to end violence against women and girls. On the International Day for the Elimination of Violence Against Women 2021, President Biden announced a renewed national plan to address gendered violence. The United Kingdom have also updated their national plan to tackle violence against women and girls (2021), which incorporates submissions from the public following the rape and murder of 33-year-old Sarah Everard by a police officer.

Here in Australia, where we reside, the government is gearing up for its fourth stage of the National Plan to Reduce Violence against Women and their Children but a series of recent events within parliament itself have raised concerns and criticism over the Government's ability to genuinely implement change. At the beginning of 2021, former staff member of the liberal party, Brittany Higgins, went public with allegations of rape by a more senior colleague in parliament house, after internal reports were met with inadequate responses. In that same year, historical allegations of rape were made against the former attorney-general, Christian

DOI: 10.4324/9781003051657-3

Porter (which he strongly denies), but to date, no independent inquiry has been pursued. A recent review also found that one in three staff in federal parliament have experienced sexual harassment (Australian Human Rights Commission 2021). Such events have left many people simmering for change in cultures that condone gendered violence, but what will be the boiling point?

Chapter 3 reflects on the political landscapes that have shaped policies regarding family violence and sexual offending (predominantly in Australia, the United States, and the United Kingdom). It examines various funding trends and the impact this has on frontline services, calling attention to the dearth of funding for women's services, especially the sexual violence sector. It considers future directions in policy frameworks for family violence and sexual offending, with a focus on data recording, corporatisation, primary prevention, and intersectionality. Finally, we discuss the impact of funding structures on the nexus between family violence and sexual offending, highlighting the implications of treating sexual offending according to a family violence framework.

The ebbs and flows of funding

Policies that address family violence and sexual violence are relatively recent in history. As highlighted in Chapter 1, it was still legal for a man to rape his wife in some states in North America until 1993, and rape within marriage is still legal in some countries such as India. In Australia, it was not until the 1970s that domestic violence began to be formally recognised and discussed by governments (Murray & Powell 2011). Prior to that, domestic violence was very much viewed as a private issue amongst couples, rather than a widespread problem requiring systematic and structural change. The 1980s saw a series of inquiries, taskforces, and reviews, highlighting domestic violence as a widespread social and economic problem. Since the 80s, however, change has been slow, with fluctuations of progress depending on various governments.

Despite increasing attention to domestic violence, conservative governments have consistently cut funding to women's services. For example, in the early 2000s the Howard government in Australia diverted 10 million dollars away from women's programmes to spend on terrorism campaigns. In 2013, the election of Tony Abbott (who appointed himself the minister for women's issues), saw the significant application of austerity measures, which forced the reduction of many frontline services for women, such as domestic violence hotlines and shelters. Similar trends were seen in other countries following global narratives of austerity and constructions of budget crises after the 2008 Global Financial Crisis (Pruitt et al. 2017).

Recently, the Morrison liberal government in Australia boasted the announcement of $22.4 million over five years to establish a Domestic, Family, and Sexual Violence Commission to oversee the implementation of the next National Plan to end violence against women and children. On the face of it, this funding is promising. But activists such as the Australian of the Year, Grace Tame, have pointed out that this funding appears to mostly serve bureaucrats and is desperately needed by existing frontline services who were already struggling to deal with the brunt of domestic violence work, even before the added impacts of the COVID-19 pandemic. The commitment also appears tokenistic following the 2020–2021's federal budget which slashed more than half of its funding for domestic and sexual violence prevention programmes for young people in schools (Hislop 2020).

Funding schemes for family and sexual violence are clearly problematic. In the United States, the Violence against Women Act (VAWA) has provided increased funding for domestic violence and sexual assault services, but agency directors still identify funding as their single most important challenge (Macy et al. 2010). Limited funding often leads to precarious employment for staff, and reduced services for victim-survivors, particularly for those from culturally and linguistically diverse backgrounds. A key part of the problem is that agencies are required to continually apply for government grants, which often have onerous and ever-changing application processes. Staff are having to spend significant amounts of time patching together funding from different sources, which diverts valuable time away from providing services to victim-survivors.

One-off funding arrangements can also lead to the sudden end of crucial services. For example, in 2020 the Federal Government in Australia completely withdrew its funding for the only national peak body for Indigenous survivors of family violence and sexual assault, as well as funding for an award-winning women's safety programme WESNET Safe Connections, which supplied secure phones to women experiencing family and sexual violence (Cross 2019). Year after year, the onus rests on organisations to prove themselves, rather than governments investing in long-term funding for programmes that are clearly vital to the community.

While we have seen the gradual move towards more coordinated and integrated approaches to family and sexual violence, distinct funding schemes can act to keep services siloed. This was evident in one of our interviews with a senior clinician in the sexual violence sector who described how clients can sometimes be passed back and forth between services depending on what issues are disclosed. For example, a child may initially be directed to a family violence service, but if sexual abuse arises as an issue, they may be sent to a separate sexual violence service that is funded to provide specialist treatment. This can clearly have implications for the experience of clients. Overall, piecemeal funding can lead to agencies working in a disjointed fashion, sometimes competing against each other for funding, despite ultimately trying to achieve the same goal.

The power of politics and funding

Funding bodies have significant influence over the remit of family violence and sexual assault services. In her book, *Decriminalizing Domestic Violence,* Leigh Goodmark points out that the majority of VAWA's funding in the United States has been allocated to the criminal legal system, and non-profit organisations are often required to collaborate with criminal legal services (e.g., law enforcement) as a condition of their funding. This has resulted in the dominance of reactive and carceral responses to family and sexual violence over social service responses and prevention initiatives. Funders also preference "innovative" measures, pressuring agencies to jump through hoops and reinvent the wheel, rather than simply funding basic and necessary services such as counselling and shelter (Macy et al. 2010).

Several of the people we interviewed in Australia also highlighted the power that funders have in shaping the work of agencies. One interviewee from the public policy sector stated, "we see agencies who started off led by women for women and end up doing basically just what they're funded to do." She also remarked that broader changes in language adopted in policy and practise (e.g., the use of family or domestic violence) can arbitrarily occur due to the language of funders, as opposed to a more meaningful reason. Another interviewee, from a regional hub of domestic and sexual violence services, described how funders and executives can influence who receives services. For example, she discussed how her agency supports male victims of domestic and sexual violence, but this was not widely advertised due to the unpopularity and hesitancy among those higher up in the agency. She elaborated that such resistance was due to concerns that those men may be using the system as part of a broader pattern of abuse against partners or family.

Importantly, funding (or lack of) plays a significant role in the response to sexual violence in conjunction with family violence services. Research with agency directors in the United States has indicated there is lack of interest in funding sexual assault services, and in turn, resources and services for sexual violence are severely compromised (Macy et al. 2010). A key challenge is that the needs of family violence victims are often immediate and at crisis-level, so family violence work takes precedence over the sexual violence aspects. As one agency director from the United States has commented: "I feel that any merger of domestic violence and sexual assault programmes will inevitably dilute the effectiveness of the sexual assault program." They went on to describe that community work to promote rape crisis services ends up on the backburner because workers are "constantly being sucked into the emergency level services of domestic violence" (Macy et al. 2010).

Similar concerns were echoed by our interviewees in Australia. One counsellor and advocate from a sexual assault service noted how her service has not seen a change in staff numbers over the past five years. But within that same timeframe, there has been significant resources pumped into the family violence sector, resulting in a three-fold increase to the staff numbers of the local family violence service. The past five years have been a significant period of change for the family violence sector in Australia. This is largely due to Australia's first Royal Commission into Family Violence which made 227 recommendations to reduce the impact of family violence in the community. The Royal Commission was established in 2015 after a series of high-profile family violence-related cases in Victoria, most notably the murder of 9-year-old Luke Batty. Luke's mother, Rosie Batty, went on to become the 2015 Australia of the year and has campaigned tirelessly for awareness and prevention of family violence. While attention to family violence was long overdue, a key concern is that it has become a juggernaut that has over-shadowed or subsumed sexual violence work. This was expressed by several of our interviewees:

> One of the biggest problems I think we have in Australia is that sexual violence is tacked on to family violence. A lot of the problem is it is only considered in one of the many actions that occurs in a family violence context. We need better recognition of sexual violence in the family context but we also need better recognition of the fact that sexual violence occurs across a range of contexts and that that's really being erased.
>
> *Dr. Rachael Burgin, Lecturer of Law and Executive Director of Rape and Sexual Assault Research and Advocacy*

> After Rosie Batty came out after the death of her son, she helped the community start a conversation about the prevalence of family violence within all levels of the community as well as the system's response. However, unfortunately sexual violence is often not recognised, as well as the impacts related to sexual violence.
>
> *Rebecca, Counsellor and Advocate at a sexual violence service*

There are several examples where sexual violence appears to be tagged onto family violence or absorbed altogether, at least in Australia. It was not until the fourth action of the National Plan to Reduce Violence against Women and their Children that sexual violence prevention was explicitly targeted. The Australian Institute of Family Studies ceased their Australian Centre for the Study of Sexual Assault, and in New South Wales, the Minister for the Prevention of Domestic and Sexual violence has at times dropped sexual violence from the portfolio. The Royal Commission into family violence dedicated a chapter in their final report to sexual violence, but sexual violence did not receive attention in its own right. There are some exceptions that buck the trend. Recently, in Geelong Victoria, the merger of two local services saw the establishment of the "Sexual Assault and Family Violence Centre," a re-branding that made an effort to emphasise sexual violence is at the forefront of their work.

So why is sexual violence so unpopular among politicians and policymakers? Over the last decade family violence has been successfully positioned as a political tool. Put simply, it looks good to address family violence. Sexual violence on the other hand is still too controversial and taboo. Dr. Burgin explained why this might be:

> If someone punches someone in the face, we can look at that and say, "that shouldn't happen", but with rape, people think rape and sex are the same, or at least very similar, and they are only the same (or at least sometimes the same) in terms of the physicality of the act. In no other way are they the same. Because everyone or most people have sex, they feel like it is too close to home and that's why its unpopular to say things like, "you should

> do something to make sure the other person is consenting", everyone goes "what if I don't do enough" – even though that's not the reality of what happens. Because that's unpopular, politicians don't want to touch it.

Interestingly, she also highlighted how sexual violence reform and prevention can sometimes be furthered under a conservative rather than a left-leaning government, as it can weave in nicely with their "tough on crime" narrative. For example, reviewing consent law can be framed as a solid move to strengthen the criminal justice system's response to sexual violence and hold offenders accountable. But working with conservative governments may be a poison chalice: while organisations might have more success in getting sexual violence on the agenda, it could come with negative consequences, such as counterproductive impacts on victim-survivors and people who have offended.

While we have been arguing that sexual violence is often lost in efforts to combat family violence, our main point is that both family violence and sexual violence sectors are under-funded, and this is unacceptable. Governments appear to lump family and sexual violence together as simply "women's issues" without treating them like the national and international emergencies that they are. For years now, scholars have pointed out that governments are quick to throw money at "national security" in efforts to keep citizens safe, without acknowledging that the real threat to lives are often men in our own communities (McCulloch et al. 2017). For example, in 2016, the Australian Government's funding for family violence paled in comparison to the budget for national security, $100 million versus $30 billion, respectively (Fitz-Gibbon et al. 2016). This is despite the fact that Australians are significantly more likely to be killed by family violence as opposed to a terrorist attack. In 2020, for example, 2 people were killed by 1 terrorist-related incident in Australia, compared to 145 people by domestic and family violence-related incidents (with on average, one woman killed per week: ABS 2021).

Similar disparities are evident in budgets for sexual violence compared to other major public health issues. For example, in the United States, government funding for sexual violence totalled $822.4 million in 2013. In the same year $1.96 billion was directed to address cardiovascular disease, $5.27 billion for cancer, $1.01 billion for diabetes, and $2.90 billion for HIV/AIDS (Waechter & Ma 2015). In other words, the total public funding to address sexual violence is a small fraction of the total funding for other health issues, even though sexual violence is more prevalent and presents a higher economic burden to the country. As Waechter and Ma point out, each year there are approximately 12 to 14 million victims of sexual violence in the United States, which is approximately 2.5 times the annual rate of cardiovascular disease, cancer, diabetes, and HIV/AIDS combined! Since the 90s the World Health Organisation has been instrumental in framing sexual violence as a public health issue but there continues to be a lag in funding commitment to address it as such.

There are clear financial incentives to address family violence and sexual offending. In the United Kingdom, for example, rape offences were estimated to cost the economy £4.8 billion in 2015–2016 (Home Office 2021). In Australia, violence against women (including family and sexual violence) was estimated to cost between $22 and $26 billion (KPMG 2016). Violence against women is one of the most significant contributors to injury, chronic disease, and premature death, which puts a huge pressure on our criminal justice and health care systems. These are clearly not just individual problems; they have major rippling impacts on the functioning of countries. How much more convincing is needed for governments to recognise the severity of these issues? What will it take for women's lives to matter? Particularly the lives of marginalised women, who are over-represented in family and sexual violence statistics.

The dearth of funding for sexual and family violence is a double disservice to women: the victim-survivors, and the workforce who are overwhelmingly women, and burnt out following the COVID-19 "shadow pandemic" of family and sexual violence cases. Many practitioners have been working tirelessly to keep up with surge of cases, often dealing with highly traumatic situations while working from home (Pfitzner, Fitz-Gibbon, & Meyer 2022). Meanwhile male-dominated industries, like the judiciary, are remunerated handsomely for engaging in services that have been proven to be largely ineffective at preventing or responding to crime, particularly family violence and sexual offending (Jordan 2011; Petrich et al. 2021; Spohn 2020). It is clear that broader patriarchal and misogynistic values are at play when it comes to funding initiatives to keep women safe.

A cornerstone of this book is that sexual violence should be recognised as a fundamental part of family violence, but this does not mean it should be addressed using the existing budgets of family violence organisations. Governments should not be receiving a "two for one deal" when it comes to the funding of family and sexual violence. Dedicated funding for sexual violence, both within and outside of family violence contexts, is needed if we are to make meaningful gains in prevention and support. Family and sexual violence are complex problems that require and deserve significant funding.

Future directions

As we move forward, there are several noteworthy trends and challenges that impact policy frameworks for family violence and sexual offending. Firstly, data collection is a seemingly innocuous but highly influential mechanism in decision-making for policies and practises. Shureeka Alves, a team leader at Kids First Australia, described to us that current data recording systems often do not accurately capture the overlapping nature of work that family and sexual violence practitioners are engaging in. In other words, a family violence case may be recorded categorically as family violence work, but the data system does not reflect that the client was also a victim-survivor of sexual violence (and vice versa for sexual violence services). She elaborated that one could manually go through case notes to qualitatively decipher the percentage of clients with overlapping needs, but overall, there is often a lack of easy access to clear data on the number of clients who have sought services for both family and sexual violence. Agency directors in the United States have also highlighted problems with data collection of services; in particular, the fact that some funders only want data for the number of new clients, rather than recognising that agencies have been working with a client multiple times (Macy et al. 2010). These are concerning trends if significant decisions about practise and culture are based on best guesses, skewed datasets, and rigid funding formulas rather than an accurate reflection of who and what is being serviced. Consulting more closely with agencies and frontline practitioners will be vital to understand what work is being done and where the real issues are.

The corporatisation of funding is another potentially concerning trend in approaches to family violence and sexual offending. Across the world we have seen the White Ribbon campaign draw attention to men's violence against women, raising millions of dollars through charity drives, community events, and workplace accreditation programmes. But the campaign, particularly the Australian branch, has seen significant criticism over recent years for being tokenistic and diverting much needed funds away from frontline services that directly help women and children. The execution of its ambassadorship programme was particularly problematic, with several ambassadors using the appointment as a cloak of good character when it became apparent they were engaging in sexist and misogynistic language, sexual harassment, and rape (Mills 2021). In 2019, the Australian arm went into liquidation after it spent more money than it raised. It was bought again in 2020 with a renewed focus on community-designed prevention, leaving many hopeful that it will not repeat its past mistakes.

In Australia, we have also seen the privatisation of national helplines for family and sexual violence. The 1800RESPECT service which provides confidential information, counselling, referral, and support for victim-survivors is now run by one of the largest private health insurance providers, through an arrangement with three women's services. This is not problematic in and of itself, but it raises questions about what we gain and lose when we have large corporate organisations running social services. Having large-scale organisations run national services has benefits in terms of reach, impact, and efficiency, but we must tread carefully and not lose sight of the original grassroots initiatives that were started by women for women. It is great to see private companies, brands, workplaces, schools, and sporting clubs take an interest in gendered violence and pledge to end violence against women, but we must ensure these motivations are genuine. Violence against women is not a passing trend. Real women and children are being raped, abused, and murdered. These matters are not to be diluted or exploited in the name of financial or reputational gain.

A more promising trend is the recognition of family violence and sexual offending as a public health epidemic, and the gradual move to primary prevention as a long-term means of preventing violence and abuse before it occurs. Countries around the world have been spurred on by the World Health Organisation's public health framework which prompts holistic approaches to violence prevention, targeting all areas of society (work, schools, media reporting). In England and Wales, this has resulted in recent investments in public awareness-raising campaigns, widespread relationships education in schools, and research into evidence-based prevention strategies. In Australia, primary prevention gained momentum with the establishment of *Our Watch*, an independent not-for-profit national organisation dedicated to the primary prevention of violence against women and children, with a focus on key actions to address gendered drivers of violence. Attention to primary prevention frameworks is encouraging, but as one of our interviewees pointed out, sometimes over-arching frameworks can lack specialist attention to specific forms of violence against women, namely, sexual violence, which requires targeted advocacy and prevention in terms of comprehensive sexual consent education. In Chapter 3, we also explore how this pattern is particularly evident for awareness-raising campaigns which touch on "disrespect" and the more palatable forms of violence against women but tend to gloss over the uncomfortable and triggering truths and the in-depth efforts needed to specifically target sexual offending within and outside of relationships.

In moving forward, it is pertinent that policy frameworks for family violence and sexual offending adopt an intersectional approach, which recognise the overlapping forms of oppression and privilege that have contributed to victim-survivors' experiences and service needs (Collins 2019). Research has indicated that budget cuts can be particularly detrimental to family violence services for culturally and linguistically diverse (CALD) clients, with shortages in qualified interpreters and translated materials and missed opportunities to engage and support young people from culturally diverse backgrounds (Pruitt et al. 2017). Rebecca, a counsellor and advocate at a sexual assault service, also raised in one of our interviews that there are still significant challenges speaking to clients with disabilities about sexual violence, especially those who have carers that are unwilling to support a client's engagement in such services. Advocacy for people with disabilities is crucial because they are over-represented as victims of sexual crime (Tidmarsh & Hamilton 2020). Rebecca also raised that her service has seen a steady rise in members of the LGBTQIA+ community, but overall, her observation is that services are still run predominantly by white, cis-gender, and heterosexual staff. Ongoing recruitment and consultation with representatives from marginalised communities and dedicated funding is clearly needed to ensure inclusive prevention strategies and services for family violence and sexual offending.

Conclusion

Over time there has been a slow evolution of political attention to family violence, and to a lesser degree sexual offending (particularly in the context of relationships). Funding is often tenuous, putting pressure on frontline services to "make do." Limited funding and distinct funding streams frequently result in the separation of policies and services to address family violence and sexual offending. Funders, policymakers, and organisations often like clear categories, but the reality is that people's lives are messy, and their experiences do not fit neatly into boxes. SR, a senior project officer in Family Violence, articulates:

> If you're in an abusive intimate partner relationship and your partner is raping you, you don't divide that in your head. You're not thinking okay now I should get this part dealt with, now I should get that part dealt with, get some help for this—it's all one big, horrible experience. I would like to see a reality centred approach across all responses – how can we best take people's real experiences and not siphon them off into different areas?

Top-down executive decisions that fail to understand the nature of abuses being dealt with can clearly have negative implications for victim-survivors. Victims do not compartmentalise their experiences, so why do we often direct them to seek help in this way? Victim-centred, coordinated approaches are key here; yet we must also be careful not to exclusively put family violence and sexual offending under the same banner and treat them as amorphously the same. There are unique nuances that require specialist intervention. While an all-encompassing approach recognises the frequent overlap of family and sexual violence, it risks losing specialist attention to sexual offending that occurs outside of family violence. As we have seen in this chapter, funding is the crux of the issue. When funding is limited, emergency family violence work takes priority and dedicated attention to sexual violence can get lost when we treat it according to a family violence framework. Throughout this book, we recommend a cross-pollination of training to boost understandings of the connections and points of disjuncture between family violence and sexual offending. This is especially true for policymakers and funders whose decisions have significant flow-on effects to our approaches to these abuses.

References

ABS. 2021. *Recorded crime – victims*. Australian Bureau of Statistics, Canberra.

Australian Human Rights Commission. 2021. *Set the standard: Report on the Independent Review into Commonwealth Parliamentary Workplaces*. Sydney.

Collins, P.H. (2019). *Intersectionality as critical social theory*. Duke University Press, Durham.

Cross, H. 2019. *Federal Government cuts funding for more domestic violence services*. National Indigenous Times, Mosman Park.

Fitz-Gibbon, K., McCulloch, J., and Maher, J. 2016. *Little in budget to counter family violence*. The Sydney Morning Herald, Sydney.

Goodmark, L., 2018. *Decriminalizing domestic violence*. University of California Press, Berkeley.

Hislop, M. 2020. *The federal government has slashed funding for its anti-domestic violence education in schools*. Women's Agenda, Melbourne.

Home Office. 2021. *Tackling violence against women and girls*. HM Government, London.

Jordan J., 2011. Here we go round the review-go-round: Rape investigation and prosecution—are things getting worse not better?. *Journal of Sexual Aggression*, 17(3), pp. 234–249. doi:10.1080/13552600.2011.613278

KPMG, (2016). *The cost of violence against women and their children in Australia*. Department of Social Services, Canberra.

Macy, R.J., Giattina, M.C., Montijo, N.J., and Ermentrout, D.M., 2010. Domestic violence and sexual assault agency directors' perspectives on services that help survivors. *Violence against Women, 16*(10), pp. 1138–1161. doi:10.1177/1077801210383085

McCulloch, J., Maher, J., Fitz-Gibbon, K., and Walklate, S. 2017. *Finally, police are taking family violence as seriously as terrorism.* The Conversation.

Mills, T. 2021. *Former White Ribbon ambassador guilty of multiple rapes unmasked.* The Age, Melbourne.

Murray, S. and Powell, A., 2011. *Domestic violence: Australian public policy.* Australian Scholarly Publishing, Melbourne.

Petrich, D.M., Pratt, T.C., Jonson, C.L., and Cullen, F.T., 2021. Custodial sanctions and reoffending: A meta-analytic review. *Crime and Justice, 50*(1), pp. 1–64. doi:10.1086/715100

Pfitzner, N., Fitz-Gibbon, K., and Meyer, S., 2022. Responding to women experiencing domestic and family violence during the COVID-19 pandemic: Exploring experiences and impacts of remote service delivery in Australia. *Child & Family Social Work, 27*(1), pp. 30–40. doi:10.1111/cfs.12870

Pruitt, L., Hamilton, G., Heydon, G., and Spark, C., 2017. Abbott's 'budget crisis', CALD women's loss? Service providers explore the impact of funding cuts. *Australian Journal of Political Science, 52*(3), pp. 335–350. doi:10.1080/10361146.2017.1332157

Spohn, C., 2020. Sexual assault case processing: The more things change, the more they stay the same. *International Journal for Crime, Justice and Social Democracy, 9*(1), pp. 86–94. doi:10.5204/ijcjsd.v9i1.1454

Tidmarsh, P. and Hamilton, G., 2020. Misconceptions of sexual crimes against adult victims: Barriers to justice. *Trends and Issues in Crime and Criminal Justice, 611*, pp. 1–18.

True, J., 2021. *Violence against women: What everyone needs to know.* Oxford University Press, Oxford.

Waechter, R. and Ma, V., 2015. Sexual violence in America: Public funding and social priority. *American Journal of Public Health, 105*(12), pp. 2430–2437. doi:10.2105/AJPH.2015.302860

3

MYTHS AND MISCONCEPTIONS OF SEXUAL OFFENDING AND FAMILY VIOLENCE

Similarities and differences

Sexual offending and family violence have now been the subject of significant research for over 40 years, developing a vast knowledge base on prevalence, offender behaviour, victim impacts, and long-term effects, and many more aspects of these crimes. The fact that they are now perceived as crimes can be put down, in part, to this increase in research and understanding. It is also clear, however, that myths and misconceptions are still present and widespread in our communities, contributing significantly to the litany of failure in developing effective responses, whether forensic, therapeutic, or preventative.

International surveys suggest that some areas of public understanding are shifting for the better. For example, in Scotland, the proportion of people who think rape within a marriage is "very seriously wrong" increased from 67% in 2014 to 84% in 2019 (Scottish Government 2020). In Australia, young people have an increasing understanding of issues concerning gender equality and violence against women, and high levels of understanding that family violence comes in many forms, not just physical abuse. Of concern, however, are continuing attitudes towards victims and high levels of errant belief in false reporting of sexual crime, maintained by one in three young men, and one in four Australian adults (Politoff et al. 2019; Webster et al. 2018). There has also been an ongoing decline in awareness that men are more likely to commit domestic violence and that women are more likely to suffer physical harm from domestic violence, which is concerning (Webster et al. 2018). Whilst such high rates of myths and misconceptions remain, all areas of policy, prevention, law, and justice responses are likely to be impacted, particularly in adversarial processes that require unanimity of decision-making "beyond reasonable doubt."

This chapter will begin with a brief overview of the history and background of myths regarding sexual offending and family violence. It provides an overview of the similarities and differences in key misconceptions about sexual offending and family violence, for both adults and children. It then explores the impact

DOI: 10.4324/9781003051657-4

of common myths on public understandings, reporting rates, justice responses, and outcomes, highlighting there is a need for more complete public awareness and prevention campaigns, to capture the connections between family violence and sexual offending.

History and background

It is impossible to consider myths and misconceptions of sexual crime and family violence without addressing the framework of structural inequalities that have created and supported them. Patriarchy and misogyny have created the systemic architecture, enshrined in law, that has made it so difficult for women and children, overwhelmingly the victims of these crimes, to tell their stories. For example, in patriarchal cultures, where women and children were considered property, rape was considered a crime against the man who was her husband, rather than an abuse of the woman herself. Men's sexual rights have been enshrined in law well into modern times. It was argued that a husband could not be guilty of rape, as the marriage contract gave him permanent consent. This argument held sway for over 200 years until debates and dissent about the law, driven by feminists in the 1970s, led to repeal. For example, in Australia, rape in marriage was finally recognised in law in 1986. In the United Kingdom, it was not recognised until 1991 (Williamson 2017), which serves as a shocking reminder of how long violence against women, at this fundamental intersection of sexual offending and family violence, has not only been tolerated, but accepted as law.

When stories of abuse do make it through the challenges of institutional exclusion, myths and misconceptions make it hard for them to be heard including the many judicial directions that significantly disadvantage complainants, some of which are now, mercifully, disappearing from the statutes. The Longman warning, for example, declared that historical delay, set arbitrarily at twenty years, meant no conviction could be considered "safe" if it relied solely on the evidence of the complainant. In many, if not most, sexual offence cases, complainants are the sole witness, and empirical evidence shows that most victim-survivors who experience rape or sexual assault delay reporting, often by many years (Commonwealth of Australia 2017; Cox 2015a). This excluded many victim-survivors from the justice system. The Crofts warning takes the notion of delayed complaint as problematic one step further, suggesting delay should be seen directly to undermine the credibility of the complainant. These examples highlight a history of structural unfairness and inequality in patriarchal law and justice processes, and the intersection between these inequalities and ignorance of the dynamics of relationship-based crime, demonstrating why so many myths and misconceptions have persisted for so long.

In the field of sexual crime, the term "rape myths" gained traction in the 70s and 80s following the ground-breaking work of feminist scholars Brownmiller (1975), Estrich (1987), and Burt (1980). Such researchers shed light on misunderstandings regarding sexual violence, and how these are often connected to broader beliefs regarding sex and gender. Work examining domestic violence myths is less established, emerging more so in the last decade. What we will see, however, is that many misconceptions regarding domestic and family violence often overlap with myths about sexual violence, but there are unique aspects as well.

Key myths and misconceptions across sexual offending and family violence

Perhaps the most important misconception that has undergone significant challenge in recent times is how prevalent sexual offending and family violence are within our communities. The taboo and hidden nature of abuse, meant for so long we did not know how many people this affected, and even when it reared its ugly head, family violence, and sexual offending were often (and still are) minimised and ignored. For example, in policing, traditionally male-dominated organisations, attention was barely given to either crime theme. Complainants were viewed with suspicion, and attrition in the early stages of investigations was very high, a figure which has changed little (Bright et al. 2021; Home Office 2019). Our current understanding of the breadth of relationship abuses, with one in three women worldwide experiencing relationship violence, including sexual offending (WHO 2021), has created advances in responses across all avenues of the service system, including policing and criminal justice. Commissions of inquiry into child sexual abuse have not only demonstrated clear evidence of the scale of abuse of children (one in five girls and one in twelve boys) but continue to reinforce the links with familial violence (Commonwealth of Australia 2017; Victorian Government 2016).

After misunderstandings of the scale of abuse, the broadest collection of misconceptions can be labelled a catalogue of victim-blaming. Sexual offending might be excused by the myriad of justifications, from provocative dress, intoxication, a lack of articulation of non-consent, or a reliance on the myth of widespread false reporting (Kelly 2010; Lisak et al. 2010; Lonsway 2010; Spohn, White & Tellis 2014; Wall & Tarczon 2013). In Australia, for example, 16% of people believe that many allegations of sexual assault made my women are false (Webster et al. 2018), when in reality, false allegations are rare (Lisak et al. 2010; Wall & Tarczon 2013).

Victim-blaming is particularly apparent in cases of sexual violence that occur within relationships. Indeed, research has found higher levels of blame attribution in acquaintance rapes, where the perpetrator was known to the victim-survivor, compared to cases classed as stranger rapes (Persson & Dhingra 2020). This flows on from the "real rape" myth, which has long been documented by scholars as the widespread belief that "real rapes" involve a stranger randomly attacking a person with a weapon, leaving behind clear physical evidence (Estrich 1987). This notion was recently demonstrated by the Governor of Texas when he expressed that, "rape is a crime, and Texas will work tirelessly to make sure that we eliminate all rapists from the streets of Texas by aggressively going out and arresting them and prosecuting them and getting them off the streets" (Bump 2021). In reality, we know that most rapes occur within the context of relationships, commonly with current or former intimate partners, behind closed doors, and without the use of violence (RAINN 2020; Waterhouse, Reynolds, & Egan 2016).

The next round of misconceptions may come about because of dominant language distancing abusive behaviours from the actions of ordinary men. Sexual crimes may be considered the acts of "monsters" (O'Hara 2012), but such misrepresents the nature of offending and offenders conjuring images of the bestial or inhuman, drawing our minds away from behaviour that should be considered endemic, common across all groups and communities. It may make us feel better to place abuse outside of human behaviour, but it surely inhibits our understanding of ourselves, and how we might best tackle these pernicious traits and behaviours. So much of our common language still places responsibility away from perpetrators, and the structures that support them, as Jane Gilmore (2019) so perfectly captures in her book (and campaign) "Fixed it," seeking to place responsibilities firmly back where they belong. For example, the headline from a mainstream newspaper, "woman was 'flirty and 'very friendly' in the hours before she was allegedly raped" is reframed by Gilmore to rightly reduce insinuations the victim is to blame and shifts the focus onto the actions of the perpetrator: "man accused of rape says alleged victim chatted to people at party."

Family violence and sexual offending also share the misconception that they always involve physical violence. For domestic and family violence, physical abuse has always been centred, although there is growing understandings that it involves psychological, emotional, financial, sexual, and verbal abuses, now recognised often as patterns of coercive control (Webster et al. 2018). Similarly, misunderstandings of sexual crime tend to over-emphasise physical violence, rather than following the research literature, which is clear that freeze behaviour and submission are far more common responses to the grooming and isolating tactics of sexual offenders (Heidt, Marx, & Forsyth 2005; Kalaf et al. 2017). Logically, then, both family violence and sexual offending misconceptions focus on lack of injuries, although from different perspectives. We may expect to see physical injuries to substantiate accounts of both sexual offending and family violence, but the nature of grooming and coercive control, and their impact on complainants, means this expectation is unlikely always to be met.

As our understanding of sexual offending and the dynamics of abusive relationships has developed, there has been an increasing focus on the relationships in which abuses occur, rather than merely a focus on the acts themselves. Notions of grooming in sexual offending, and coercive control in family violence, highlight the critical phases of developing abuses, and the background of power and control. They also expose the driving behaviours of perpetrators, fracturing the myths of shared responsibility, and allowing investigators to understand the breadth of evidence available to them, and develop offender-focused investigations, to replace the traditional models which so often concentrated on the behaviour of complainants.

The focus on offender behaviour and the development of an abusive "relationship" has begun to make inroads into misconceptions of delay in complaint, lack of injuries or resistance, as well as continued relationships with alleged perpetrators. Indeed, understandings of grooming and coercive control in abusive relationships, have helped to address the question so commonly asked of victim-survivors in both family violence and sexual offending relationships, "why didn't she just leave?" This question strikes to the heart of all these crimes, misunderstanding the nature and impact of these abusive relationship practises, making it almost impossible for victim-survivors to simply leave in a safe manner. Frameworks of grooming and coercive control, and subsequent understandings of why victims delay reporting, may also impact views on false reporting, so long a part of dismissing victims' stories. Whilst myths of false reporting still hold influence in our communities, there is some evidence that they are on the wane, at least in some jurisdictions, driven by public campaigns, such as #MeToo, educational information from the victim services sector, and academic research (ABC 2019; Scottish Government 2020).

Deeper understandings of grooming and coercive control may also be impacting misconceptions about abuses that occur in close proximity to others, an accusation often ignored as implausible. The hidden nature of abuses, even hidden "in plain sight," can now be readily understood in the nexus of offender behaviour, the predominance of abuse within intimate relationships, and victims' justifiable fears of meeting a lack of understanding, from both their immediate community and the justice system, should they come forward to report.

Complainant memory, so critical to investigations and prosecutions of sexual offending and family violence, where their narrative usually represents the only evidence, has long been the subject of misconception, a fact defence counsel use to their advantage in court (Zyderveldt et al. 2017). Recent scientific advances in understanding memory, and traumatic memory (Goodman-Delahunty, Nolan, & Van Gijn 2017; Hardy, Young, & Holmes 2009; LaBar & Cabeza 2006; Levine 2015), have led to changes in many areas of investigation and prosecution, including forensic interviewing training, investigative methodology, non-particularised charging, and expectations of giving evidence in court, to name but a few.

Given the intersectional and structural inequalities established over many years, it is not surprising that sexual offending and family violence have so many connected myths and misconceptions. Even this brief analysis of myths and misconceptions (see AIFS & Victoria Police 2017 and Tidmarsh & Hamilton 2020 for more comprehensive lists), shows how many myths and misconceptions are connected to both sexual offending and family violence: diminishing prevalence, emphasising provocation, prioritising stranger assaults, expecting immediate reporting, expecting high rates of falsity, disbelieving abuse occurring in close proximity to others, and doubting complainants' memories, all connect the two.

Despite the overwhelming similarities of myths and misconceptions across sexual offending and family violence, there are some differences. The term family violence obviously denotes an understanding that all abuses occur within the context of relationship, so misconceptions about the predominance of stranger abuses does not correlate to sexual offending myths, where the phenomenon still exists. Instead, in family violence, the myths concentrate on the issues of who is the victim, with some arguing that men are abused as frequently as women, which assertion runs significantly at odds with research evidence and police statistics (ABS 2021; ONS 2018; RAINN 2020).

It is also evident that different aspects of victim-blaming myths are drawn upon depending on whether violence occurs within or outside of relationships. For example, victims of stranger rapes may be blamed on the basis they did not take enough responsibility for their safety (e.g., they shouldn't have been out at night, they shouldn't have been walking alone, they were intoxicated); victims of acquaintance rapes may be blamed for "misleading" perpetrators through what they wore or how they communicated non-consent; and victims of intimate partner sexual violence may be blamed for their choice of partner, whose actions are justified because consent is viewed as ongoing within relationships. Even when rapes within relationships are recognised, people may lean on the belief it does not cause much harm to victims (Scottish Government 2020), despite evidence victim-survivors report intimate partner sexual violence as one of the most damaging forms of abuse (Tarzia 2020). Whichever shade of myth is relied upon, it is clear each is entangled within the broader frameworks of patriarchy, sexism, and misogyny, and can have significant impacts for victim-survivors and justice responses, which we will explore in further sections of this chapter. First let us consider some myths that pertain specifically to children.

Children

Understandings of child sexual abuse have developed rapidly in the last few decades, much of it deriving from a focus on offenders. Our knowledge of grooming and the manipulations of trust and relationship used by offenders has allowed us a greater awareness of children's experiences of abuse. Consequently, many assumptions and misconceptions have been challenged, though some persist. The same cannot be said of children experiencing family violence, so long assumed to be witnesses, rather than victims, with physical abuse of children almost seen as a separate experience altogether. It is not until more recent times that they have begun to be acknowledged as victims of both the violence itself, and the other elements of family violence we now recognise, particularly psychological and emotional abuses. It has taken even longer for us to consider the relationship between sexual offending against children and family violence, with relatively few studies, even now, considering the connections. This connection will be explored further in Chapter 5.

In addressing myths and misconceptions, children, and our beliefs and attitudes towards them, deserve special mention. They suffer both from some of the same misconceptions as adults, but also others related to their youth itself. The related misconceptions derive from the same historical issues of patriarchal structure, and assumptions regarding the way they should have behaved when experiencing abuse from trusted adults. Differences centre on the unreliability of children as witnesses and doubts about their memories. It is important to note here, of course, that most children do not report their abuse in childhood, if at all. The Royal Commission into Institutional Responses to Child Sexual Abuse found that survivors took an average of 22 years to report their abuse (Commonwealth of Australia 2017).

In conversation with a prosecutor, some decade or so ago, I (Tidmarsh) asked if anything had changed, in recent times, in the way they went about their business. Their reply was that the biggest shift had come in not having to persuade juries that child sexual abuse exists, which surprised me. It was not until I realised how onerous the adversarial system is, in requiring unanimity of thought from fact finders, that I realised what a relief that knowledge must have been to the prosecutor. We are now realising that child sexual abuse is widespread, as are rape, sexual assault, and sexual harassment. However, I still find, in almost every group I talk to, that people are shocked at how common sexual offending and family violence are in our communities. There is also shock when we discuss the next element, of who the perpetrators are and what relationship they typically have with those they victimise.

Even more so than with adults, we have traditionally emphasised the risks strangers pose to children, despite developing evidence of the relatively small percentage of offending by strangers, with close male figures, the overwhelming proportion of perpetrators (RAINN 2021). This misunderstanding has led to the same attacks on children's credibility as it has with adults, but they appear even more absurd here. Misperceptions that children would immediately report abuse to a trusted adult, when that adult was probably the perpetrator, or related to the perpetrator, demonstrate the challenges of reporting abuse for any child. Notions of resistance, and of unequivocal negative feelings towards the perpetrator, also seem profoundly unrealistic in the context of relationship abuse. Similarly, understanding where abuse takes place and who the perpetrators are shows that disbelief about offending happening in close proximity to others is unfounded. Even when children are abused by those outside their families, offending can still take place in close proximity to others (ABS 2017; Larsen et al. 2015; Waterhouse et al. 2016).

Children, in line with women, are plagued with the myth that they make up false stories about sexual offending, and their words alone cannot be trusted. This notion was famously expressed by Lord Chief Justice Hale in the 17th century when he said that a rape allegation is "easily to be made and hard to be proved, and harder to be defended by the party accused" (Eastwood, Kift, & Grace 2006). This sentiment has been echoed over time by lawyers and judges, cementing itself into contemporary law, academic literature, and practises of investigation. Indeed, one law journal article, as recently as 2009, expressed the view that children are as capable as adults of malicious allegation and lying about sexual abuse (Coyle et al. 2009), despite evidence that children hardly ever lie about sexual abuse (Everson & Boat 1989; O'Donohue, Cummings, & Willis 2018). In the practises of relationship-based crime investigation, so dependent on the narratives of complainants as evidence, much time is spent on assessing the ability of children to articulate the difference between truth and lies, whether they are four or fifteen. Whilst it is an understandable question to ask, it has traditionally been done as if the likelihood of falsity is high, often coming before children have even begun their disclosure. The argument was that time would be saved if problems were found at the earliest point, but the impression children may receive is that they are unlikely to be believed. Such practises are a long way from "victim-centred" and "trauma-informed" practise. Even the scepticism often levelled at adult complainants does not appear so strongly here, with questions such as, "and is everything you have said today the truth?" asked at the end of interviews or the taking of written statements.

Finally, the notion of children as poor witnesses, with unreliable memories, has had a profound effect on investigation and prosecution of child sexual abuse and family violence, and most particularly the former. Evidence that children as young as four can remember events accurately (Wilson & Powell 2001), improvements in the forensic interviewing of children, and the introduction of intermediaries have all improved our understanding of how children remember, and talk about, their experiences of abuse. The law is finally changing here too, as explained by the Australian Law Reform Commission, in its notes on the Uniform Evidence Act, "18.2: Warnings about the potential unreliability of categories of witnesses such as women and children are now recognised as discriminatory and based on prejudice rather than empirical evidence."

The impact of myths and misconceptions

Courts play a vital role in our understanding of what is just and what is "true." However, not only have stories of sexual offending and family violence had a hard time reaching our courts, once there, conviction rates have always been low (Daly & Bouhours 2010). They are most notable for sexual offences, as the focus of investigations is exclusively forensic. In recent years, despite significant increases in reporting, convictions for sexual offences have sunk even lower (The Centre for Women's Justice et al. 2020). Myths and misconceptions play a vital role here, as jury decisions must be reached beyond any reasonable doubt. Given the complexity of community thinking and values around sexual behaviour, many cases may not present a reasonable prospect of conviction, as misconceptions create doubt. Indeed, research indicates that myths held by jurors, particularly around what is considered "real rape" can impact their evaluation of the evidence and their decision-making in sexual offence cases (Leverick 2020).

Rape myths are routinely employed in sexual offence trials (Skinner & Smith 2017). Recent research into rape trials, contrasting contemporary trials with those 50 years prior, suggests little has changed in the overall tactics employed to undermine complainant's accounts, but there are some encouraging signs of shifts in attitudes. Defence counsel, whilst still attacking complainants' credibility as their core strategy, can no longer rely on protestations of the suspect's good character, attacks on the sexual history of the complainant, or sly suggestions that her lack of injuries says she did not resist and was therefore willing. Instead, recent attacks are more likely to concern delays in reporting, continued relationship with the perpetrator, or problems with memory (Zyderveldt et al. 2017). Despite advances to our understanding of grooming and coercive control, awareness of known parties as the offenders, and that traumatised memories require expert interviewing, these tactics are still abound.

Misconceptions about sexual crime may contribute to other problems, including case attrition earlier on in the criminal justice process. Community views and stigma may influence initial reporting rates (Weiss 2010). Indeed, the highest attrition of all comes before anyone has told their story, evidenced by the extremely low reporting rates for sexual offending and family violence, mere fractions of the overall rates (ABS 2021). There is a myriad of reasons why victim-survivors do not report abuse: shame, fear of the perpetrator, a mistrust of police, and a fear they will not be believed. Non-reporting can also stem from misunderstandings of their experiences, particularly their sense of responsibility and self-blame. For example, in Australia, 74% of female sexual assault victim-survivors did not immediately realise they have been assaulted, suggesting significant misunderstandings about what sexual violence entails (ABS 2021). This is perhaps even more true for victims of intimate partner sexual violence. Research indicates that women are less likely to report intimate partner sexual violence than non-sexual physical assault by an intimate partner and tend to only report the most severe cases of intimate partner sexual violence to police (Cox 2015b).

Even once a victim-survivor has overcome the enormous barriers to reporting, myths impact police judgements of a victim's credibility and, in turn, their investigations and decision-making (Tidmarsh, Hamilton, & Sharman 2020). Legal professionals, who make decisions about whether a case proceeds through the criminal justice system, base their perceptions and expectations about whether it will result in a guilty verdict on the basis of whether there is a "reasonable prospect" of reaching a conviction. These perceptions may be heavily influenced by their own misconceptions, or beliefs about misconceptions held by fact finders the case will encounter later in the justice process. This thinking may lead to decisions based on guesswork, and fact finders' views based on their own experiences, rather than the merits of the case itself, which phenomenon has been referred to as downstream orientation (Frohmann 1997; Pattavina, Morabito, & Williams 2016). In terms of sexual offence cases, we see these misconceptions play out in higher arrest rates for suspects who are strangers compared to those known to the victim, whether acquaintance or intimate partner (Morabito, Williams, & Pattavina 2019).

With our understanding of family violence and sexual crime imagined, or gained through mainstream media (O'Hara 2012), many research findings may struggle to break through to the public's consciousness. This can have impacts, not only on our criminal justice responses, but also on public health policies and prevention initiatives. For example, messages to young women about protecting themselves when out in public, fuelled by dreadful assaults and murders, ignore the overwhelming evidence that they are far more at risk from the men they are in relationship with. Traditional messages to children, about being most aware of the dangers posed by strangers, fly in the face of clear evidence that child sexual abuse is often perpetrated by a close male role model or family member. Research also indicates that such offending, over long timeframes, and involving penetrative offending, has significant links to poor later mental health outcomes, including higher rates of schizophrenic and psychotic disorders (Cutajar et al. 2010), suggesting such misconceptions not only misinform children and parents, but may impact funding and policy in critical areas of mental health.

Conclusions and future directions

Our understanding of sexual offending and family violence has improved markedly in recent times, from increased public awareness campaigns, practitioners, researchers, and advocates with lived experience. There are clear signs that this is having a positive impact and reducing myths and misconceptions of both sexual crime and family violence in our communities (Scottish Government 2020), although not all attitudes are heading in a positive direction (Webster et al. 2018). Despite significant funding for services and widespread public attention, family and sexual violence are still misunderstood and underreported. The practises of investigation, prosecution, and court process have all made improvements and yet, despite significant rises in reporting, case attrition remains high, and conviction rates have been declining in sexual offence cases (Daly & Bouhours 2010; Lovett & Kelly 2009). The nexus between reporting, attrition, and conviction rates emphasises the need for change in every aspect of our responses, from encouraging reporting and supporting victims, to finding appropriate and effective justice responses. In terms of myths and misconceptions, reporting remains a vital marker of change, as victims will only come forward to tell a community, and justice system, that will listen. Our aim must be to eradicate myths and misconceptions of family and sexual violence from our attitudes and beliefs, but it appears we still have some way to go.

Whilst it is encouraging to see individual misconceptions recede, it is vital to keep an eye on the central misconceptions, which lead us to write this book, that family violence and sexual offending are either one and the same, or entirely separate, rather than separate but overlapping constructs. It is clear that public constructions and conceptualisations of family violence and sexual offending are having impacts on community attitudes and perceptions, disclosure and reporting, investigation, adjudication, and justice outcomes, particularly for cases of intimate partner sexual violence. If public campaigns focus just on sexual violence in particular contexts, other forms of sexual violence will remain more hidden. If family violence campaigns, which are often sterile and discursive, never explicitly address sexual violence, people might not recognise this abuse in relationships. This is a clear avenue of future research. How can we promote more nuanced understandings of family and sexual violence to ensure justice and healing for all types of abuses, whether they fall within or outside of the dominant stereotypes of family violence and sexual offending?

It is also clear that public understandings and media representations still focus on violence within heteronormative relationships. Future research needs to focus on how myths impact under-represented groups, such as LGBTQIA+ people, First Nations people, migrant communities, and people with disabilities. It is only through more diverse understandings and fuller prevention campaigns that we will be able to create futures free of violence for everyone.

References

ABC News, 2019. Australia talks: Data explorer. www.abc.net.au/news/2020-12-10/australia-talks-data-explorer-2019/12946988#/

ABS, 2017. *Personal safety survey, Australia 2016.* Australian Bureau of Statistics, Canberra.

ABS, 2021. *Recorded crime – victims.* Australian Bureau of Statistics, Canberra.

AIFS & Victoria Police, 2017. *Challenging misconceptions about sexual offending: Creating an evidence-based resource for police and legal practitioners.* Australian Institute of Family Studies, Melbourne.

Bright, S., Roach, C., Barnaba, L., Walker, S., and Millsteed, M., 2021. *Attrition of sexual offence incidents through the Victorian criminal justice system.* Crime Statistics Agency, Melbourne.

Brownmiller, S., 1975. *Against our will: Men, women, and rape.* Fawcett Book, New York.

Bump, P., 2021. *Texas's governor pledges to try to 'eliminate all rapists' to prevent rape-related abortions.* The Washington Post, Washington.

Burt, M.R., 1980. Cultural myths and supports for rape. *Journal of Personality and Social Psychology, 38*(2), pp. 217–230. doi:10.1037/0022-3514.38.2.217

Commonwealth of Australia, 2017. *Royal commission into institutional responses to child sexual abuse: Final report.* Canberra.

Cox, P., 2015a. *Violence against women in Australia: Additional analysis of the Australian Bureau of Statistics' Personal Safety Survey, 2012.* Australia's National Research Organisation for Women's Safety, Sydney.

Cox, P., 2015b. *Sexual assault and domestic violence in the context of co-occurrence and re-victimisation State of knowledge.* ANROWS, Sydney.

Coyle, I.R., Field, D., Wilson, P., Cuthbert, C., and Miller, G., 2009. Out of the mouths of babes: The case for an increased use of expert evidence in rebuttal of sexual abuse allegations by child witnesses. *Criminal Law Journal, 33*(3), pp. 139–164.

Cutajar, M.C., Mullen, P.E., Ogloff, J.R., Thomas, S.D., Wells, D.L., and Spataro, J., 2010. Schizophrenia and other psychotic disorders in a cohort of sexually abused children. *Archives of General Psychiatry, 67*(11), pp. 1114–1119. doi:10.1001/archgenpsychiatry.2010.147

Daly, K. and Bouhours, B., 2010. Rape and attrition in the legal process: A comparative analysis of five countries. *Crime and Justice, 39*(1), pp. 565–650. doi:10.1086/653101

Estrich, S., 1987. *Real rape. How the legal system victimizes women who say no.* Harvard University Press, Cambridge.

Everson, M.D. and Boat, B.W., 1989. False allegations of sexual abuse by children and adolescents. *Journal of the American Academy of Child & Adolescent Psychiatry, 28*(2), pp. 230–235.

Frohmann, L., 1997. Convictability and discordant locales: Reproducing race, class, and gender ideologies in prosecutorial decision-making. *Law and Society Review*, pp. 531–556. doi:3054045

Gilmore, J., 2019. *Fixed it: Violence and the representation of women in the media.* Viking Press, New York.

Goodman-Delahunty, J., Nolan, M.A., and Van Gijn, E.L., 2017. *Empirical guidance on the effects of child sexual abuse on memory and complainants' evidence.* Royal Commission into Institutional Responses to Child Sexual Abuse, Canberra.

Hardy, A., Young, K., and Holmes, E.A., 2009. Does trauma memory play a role in the experience of reporting sexual assault during police interviews? An exploratory study. *Memory, 17*(8), pp. 783–788. doi:10.1080/09658210903081835

Heidt, J.M., Marx, B.P., and Forsyth, J.P., 2005. Tonic immobility and childhood sexual abuse: A preliminary report evaluating the sequela of rape-induced paralysis. *Behaviour Research and Therapy, 43*(9), pp. 1157–1171. doi: 10.1016/j.brat.2004.08.005

Home Office, 2019. *Crime outcomes in England and Wales: Year ending March 2019, Statistical Bulletin HOSB 12/19.* U.K. Government, London.

Kalaf, J., Coutinho, E.S.F., Vilete, L.M.P., Luz, M.P., Berger, W., Mendlowicz, M., Volchan, E., Andreoli, S.B., Quintana, M.I., de Jesus Mari, J., and Figueira, I., 2017. Sexual trauma is more strongly associated with tonic immobility than other types of trauma: A population based study. *Journal of Affective Disorders, 215*, pp. 71–76. doi:10.1016/j.jad.2017.03.009

Kelly, L., 1988. *Surviving sexual violence.* John Wiley & Sons, Cambridge.

Kelly, L., 2010. The (in) credible words of women: False allegations in European rape research. *Violence Against Women, 16*(12), pp. 1345–1355. doi:10.1177/1077801210387748

LaBar, K.S. and Cabeza, R., 2006. Cognitive neuroscience of emotional memory. *Nature Reviews Neuroscience,* 7(1), pp. 54–64. doi:10.1038/nrn1825

Larsen, M.L., Hilden, M., and Lidegaard, Ø., 2015. Sexual assault: A descriptive study of 2500 female victims over a 10-year period. *BJOG: An International Journal of Obstetrics & Gynaecology, 122*(4), pp. 577–584. doi:10.1111/1471-0528.13093

Leverick, F., 2020. What do we know about rape myths and juror decision making?. *The International Journal of Evidence & Proof, 24*(3), pp. 255–279. doi:10.1177/1365712720923157

Levine, P.A., 2015. *Trauma and memory: Brain and body in a search for the living past: A practical guide for understanding and working with traumatic memory.* North Atlantic Books, Berkeley.

Lisak, D., Gardinier, L., Nicksa, S.C., and Cote, A.M., 2010. False allegations of sexual assault: An analysis of ten years of reported cases. *Violence against Women, 16*(12), pp. 1318–1334. doi:10.1177/1077801210387747

Lonsway, K.A., 2010. Trying to move the elephant in the living room: Responding to the challenge of false rape reports. *Violence against Women, 16*(12), pp. 1356–1371. doi:10.1177/1077801210387750

Lovett, J. and Kelly, L., 2009. *Different systems, similar outcomes? Tracking attrition in reported rape cases across Europe.* Child and Women Abuse Studies Unit, London Metropolitan University, London.

Morabito, M., Williams, L., and Pattavina, A., 2019. *Decision making in sexual assault cases: Replication research on sexual violence case attrition in the U.S.* National Institute of Justice, U.S. Department of Justice, Washington DC.

O'Donohue, W., Cummings, C., and Willis, B., 2018. The frequency of false allegations of child sexual abuse: A critical review. *Journal of Child Sexual Abuse, 27*(5), pp. 459–475. doi:10.1080/10538712.2018.1477224

O'Hara, S., 2012. Monsters, playboys, virgins and whores: Rape myths in the news media's coverage of sexual violence. *Language and Literature, 21*(3), pp. 247–259. doi:10.1177/0963947012444217

ONS, 2018. *Sexual offending: Victimisation and the path through the criminal justice system.* Office for National Statistics, London.

Pattavina, A., Morabito, M., and Williams, L.M., 2016. Examining connections between the police and prosecution in sexual assault case processing: Does the use of exceptional clearance facilitate a downstream orientation?. *Victims & Offenders, 11*(2), pp. 315–334. doi:10.1080/15564886.2015.1046622

Persson, S. and Dhingra, K., 2020. Attributions of blame in stranger and acquaintance rape: A multilevel meta-analysis and systematic review. *Trauma, Violence, & Abuse*, pp. 1–15. doi:10.1177/1524838020977146

Politoff, V., Crabbe, M., Honey, N., Mannix, S., Mickle, J., Morgan, J., Parkes, A., Powell, A., Stubbs, J., Ward, A., and Webster, K., 2019. *Young Australians' attitudes to violence against women and gender equality: Findings from the 2017 National Community Attitudes towards Violence against Women Survey (NCAS)*. Australia's National Research Organisation for Women's Safety (ANROWS), Sydney.

RAINN, 2020. *Victims of sexual violence—Statistics*. Rape, Abuse & Incest National Network, Washington.

RAINN, 2021. *Children and teens: Statistics*. Rape, Abuse & Incest National Network, Washington.

Scottish Government, 2020. *Scottish Social Attitudes Survey 2019: Attitudes to violence against women*. Social Research, Edinburgh.

Smith, O. and Skinner, T., 2017. How rape myths are used and challenged in rape and sexual assault trials. *Social & Legal Studies, 26*(4), pp. 441–466. doi:10.1177/0964663916680130

Spohn, C., White, C., and Tellis, K., 2014. Unfounding sexual assault: Examining the decision to unfound and identifying false reports. *Law & Society Review, 48*(1), pp. 161–192. doi:10.1111/lasr.12060

Tarzia, L., 2020. "It went to the very heart of who I was as a woman": The invisible impacts of intimate partner sexual violence. *Qualitative Health Research, 31*(2), pp. 287–297. doi:10.1177/1049732320967659

The Centre for Women's Justice, End Violence against Women, Imkaan, and Rape Crisis England and Wales. 2020. *The decriminalisation of rape: Why the justice system is failing rape survivors and what needs to change*. England and Wales.

Tidmarsh, P. and Hamilton, G., 2020. Misconceptions of sexual crimes against adult victims: Barriers to justice. *Trends and Issues in Crime and Criminal Justice, 611*, pp. 1–18.

Tidmarsh, P., Hamilton, G., and Sharman, S.J., 2020. Changing police officers' attitudes in sexual offense cases: A 12-month follow-up study. *Criminal Justice and Behavior, 47*(9), pp. 1176–1189. doi:10.1177/0093854820921201

Victorian Government, 2016. *Royal Commission into family violence: Summary and recommendations*. RCFV, Victoria.

Wall, L. and Tarczon, C., 2013. *True or false? The contested terrain of false allegations*. Australian Institute of Family Studies, Melbourne.

Waterhouse, G.F., Reynolds, A., and Egan, V., 2016. Myths and legends: The reality of rape offences reported to a UK police force. *The European Journal of Psychology Applied to Legal Context, 8*(1), pp. 1–10. doi:10.1016/j.ejpal.2015.04.001

Webster, K., Diemer, K., Honey, N., Mannix, S., Mickle, J., Morgan, J., Parkes, A., Politoff, V., Powell, A., Stubbs, J., and Ward, A., 2018. *2017 National Community Attitudes towards Violence against Women Survey (NCAS): methodology report*. Australia's National Research Organisation for Women's Safety (ANROWS), Sydney.

Weiss, K.G., 2010. Too ashamed to report: Deconstructing the shame of sexual victimization. *Feminist Criminology, 5*(3), pp. 286–310. doi:10.1177/1557085110376343

WHO, 2021. *Violence against Women Prevalence Estimates, 2018*. World Health Organisation, Geneva.

Williamson, A., 2017. The law and politics of marital rape in England, 1945–1994. *Women's History Review, 26*(3), pp. 382–413. doi:10.1080/09612025.2015.1133536

Wilson, C. and Powell, M., 2001. *A guide to interviewing children: Essential skills for counsellors, police lawyers and social workers*. Routledge, New York. doi:10.4324/9780203390023

Zydervelt, S., Zajac, R., Kaladelfos, A., and Westera, N., 2017. Lawyers' strategies for cross-examining rape complainants: Have we moved beyond the 1950s?. *British Journal of Criminology*, *57*(3), pp. 551–569. doi:10.1093/bjc/azw023

4

POLICING AND INVESTIGATIVE RESPONSES TO FAMILY VIOLENCE AND SEXUAL OFFENCES

This chapter explores how policing might develop to respond to the most pernicious of crimes: family violence and sexual offending. It begins with an overview of policing cultures and developments in recent times, particularly in the context of Victoria, Australia. Next, we turn to key differences in investigative approaches, and challenges related to police discretion, interviewing, evidence-gathering, and prosecuting. We outline the Whole Story investigative methodology and build the case for specialist, trauma-informed, and victim-centric approaches to policing family violence and sexual crimes, along with the potential for relationship-based crime commands in police services. We argue that improved responses, in recent times, are still driven by too many assumptions, rather than by research knowledge, and that while there is a strong case for shared practice, some key differences between family violence and sexual offences require a continued specialism in each area.

Policing culture and context

Policing has come a long way, in recent times, in its responses to sexual offending and family violence. In Victoria, where we both work, the two seminal reports detailing the need for change were the 2004 Victorian Law Reform Commission (VLRC) into how state services responded to sexual offending, particularly its treatment of victim-survivors, and the 2015 Victorian Royal Commission in Family Violence (RCFV; Victorian Government 2016). Each report called for change, but the tone of criticism and recommendation was noticeably different, particularly in relation to policing. In 2004, the VLRC was scathing about the force's "cultures of disbelief," critiquing attitudes and practices, suggesting that police lacked subject matter specialism, and that they did not have the confidence of the public. The RCFV, whilst calling for change in its 227 recommendations, made no such damning assessment of police culture and attitudes. Two other reports, from 2015,

DOI: 10.4324/9781003051657-5

showed how far policing of sexual crime had come in the decade since VLRC, and how difficult it is for poor policing culture and attitudes to change. The Victim Support Agency (VSA 2015) found that, far from the dark days before the VLRC, victims of sexual crime were one of the most satisfied of any reporting group with their experience of police, at least in Victoria in 2015. The Victorian Human Rights and Equal Opportunity Commission (VHREOC 2015), by contrast, found that many police themselves were far from satisfied with their own organisation, detailing high rates of sexual harassment and bullying. VHREOC also suggested that police do not exist in a vacuum, rather representing the same attitudes, beliefs, and behaviours as the wider community.

Police cultures have been described as, "hyper-masculine, results-oriented, emotionally detached, loyal, insular, hierarchical, authoritarian and hostile to the scrutiny of outsiders" (Rich & Seffrin 2014). It is no surprise then, that crime themes like sexual offending and family violence, disproportionately affecting women and children, and with a poor history of effectiveness in achieving results, have only recently become priorities in policing agendas. The work was seen to have little value, with "elite squads" focused on stranger rapes and organised child exploitation, rather than addressing most sexual crimes, occurring between known parties, typically in relationships. Family violence fared little better, called "domestics" or "domestic disputes," suggesting violence was minor, or barely a crime. Police practices also suffered from the myriad of myths and misconceptions that abound on these subjects: misunderstanding continued relationships between perpetrator and victim, delays in reporting, gaps in memory, lack of visible injury, reluctance to make statements, and many other issues that could have been understood had policing read the science and listened to victims. All these misconceptions contributed to the relegation of relationship-based crime to the bottom of the list of priorities. Here, again, is a strong link to broader societal attitudes and beliefs, where the "downstream orientation" effect, of predicting jurors' thinking, led police and prosecutors to weed out all but the most easily understood scenarios (Pattavina, Morabito, & Williams 2016). Even now, particularly in sexual crime cases, attrition remains high and conviction rates very low (Bright et al. 2021; Daly & Bouhours 2010). On a more practical, and perhaps more understandable, note, the practises of policing, so often driven by statistical analyses of "volume" crime, could not see the value in putting resources into investigations and prosecutions that were time consuming and unlikely to result in convictions.

Moves to make policing more victim-centric and trauma-informed have needed to understand the barriers in both police and community attitudes. These barriers are more widespread and pervasive than specific misconceptions of victim and offender behaviour, mired in the deeper and more entrenched issues of patriarchal thought and community structures, misogyny, homophobia, and racism. Policing has not just been "hyper-masculine," but also mostly white. People, particularly women and children, outside the dominant cultural groups, are more likely to be offended against, less likely to report, and less likely to have their case heard in court (AIHW 2019; Martin et al. 2006; MoJ 2013). The LGBTQIA+ community face similar issues (Rothman, Exner, & Baughman 2011; WHO 2002; Walters, Chen, & Breiding 2011). VHREOC also found high rates of homophobia, making it difficult to be "out" in policing cultures. People with disabilities, who are much more likely to be targeted by offenders than those living without disability, not only face significant hurdles in reporting, but are much more likely to have their story thought of as a false report (Murray & Heenan 2012; Murray & Powell 2008). To be genuinely victim-centric and trauma-informed, policing is having to come to terms with all these inequalities, and community attitudes and beliefs, not just the myths and misconceptions relevant to sexual crime and family violence. If victims of sexual crime and family violence, subjected to the trauma of abuse, were to look at traditional police forces that do not reflect their diversity, why would they choose to report at all?

It is no coincidence, therefore, that changes have come as women have taken up more and more senior roles in policing, although recruiting people of colour and First Nations people has not been so successful. In Victoria, the VLRC (2004) coincided with the first female Chief Commissioner of Police, Christine Nixon, who was quick to establish initiatives to improve responses to sexual offending and family violence (SSCRSA 2006; SSCRFV 2006). Since that time, initiatives have come thick and fast, with specialist investigators, multi-disciplinary centres, and improved risk assessments, accompanied by increased funding and specialist training. Having acknowledged that policing has long failed adequately to address sexual offending and family violence, the changes that have come about recently have caused problems too, particularly with the developing debate about how policing sexual offences and family violence intersects. Changes have come about so fast across the sector that one manager, working in the nexus between sexual offending and family violence, described their role as "like flying the plane while it's still being built."

Different approaches to policing family violence and sexual crime

Whatever attempts there are to coordinate policing across different crime themes, and despite so many similarities between offenders and in their impact on victims, there are significant differences in the way sexual offending and family violence are policed, most of which are unlikely to change. Four stand out.

Firstly, despite delays in reporting family violence, as is the case with almost all sexual offences, the tipping point of any report means that police respond when matters are *in crisis.* Victims reporting sexual offending seldom do so in a crisis. Research shows that, for both kinds of abuse, particularly sexual abuses, immediate reporting is the exception rather than the rule, with only about 5% of sexual crime victims reporting to authorities within 72 hours of the offence (a timeframe typically used by police to determine an "immediate report").[1] Whilst family violence is also under-reported, with delayed reporting also typical, the point of reporting is often brought about by acts of violence, or threat, leading to a crisis point that provokes the report. So, at the point of reporting, as one senior officer put, when police respond to that crisis point, "family violence trumps everything," by which he meant that the requirements for safe resolution of the presenting crisis, and the priorities of risk assessment and safety planning take precedence over everything else, and rightly so. What this means, in practise, is that investigative priorities, even in relation to violence, never mind the exploration of sexual offending, take secondary importance. This is so, even if it alerts the offender to police involvement, which can have detrimental effects on any subsequent investigation. Risk assessment, itself, provides a key difference here too, and a potential opportunity for future policing practise. Currently, family violence investigations focus heavily on risk assessment, as discussed, but risk assessment carries no such overwhelming imperative in sexual offence allegations. That is not to say it is not important, particularly when the victim is a child, but rather that risk is not the main driver of the process, but rather the process of investigation. As we will see further in Chapter 5, the connections between family violence, sexual assault, and child sexual abuse are becoming clearer and clearer. When it comes to responding to disclosures of family violence, current procedures prioritise risk assessment. Although one might have thought that initial risk assessment of the family violence would be beneficial to any future investigations, this is far less likely to be the case with allegations of sexual offences, if indeed the risk assessment elicits such allegations at all. Current risk assessments for family violence, even when police forces have them, often make little mention of potential sexual offending, whether against adults or children. This is so despite evidence of the clear links between family violence and sexual assault, and between family violence and child sexual abuse (Bagwell-Grey, Messing, & Baldwin-White 2015; Bidarra, Lessard, & Dumont 2016). It is so even though sexual assault in violent relationships is the highest single risk factor for femicide (Campbell et al. 2017). The current risk assessment model in Victoria has only one question that asks about adult sexual assault. As interviewing is a complex task and asking about such personal matters is challenging on many levels, sometimes it is not even asked.

When investigators, whether uniform or detectives, hear a victim's report, their first job, as police manuals will tell them, is to determine whether a crime has been committed. Previously, the biggest problem with this instruction was that, rather than seeing the report as the beginning of eliciting a narrative and ascertaining potential avenues of enquiry, police were just as likely to find fault with the victim, assume the complaint would go nowhere, or see it as a false report. Now, with changes to culture and practice developing rapidly, the biggest concern is that investigators might ask themselves, "which crime?," and concentrate on the most obvious answer, rather than seeing the possible complexity of any given situation. It may seem, given the likelihood of more tangible, visible evidence, that family violence is easier to investigate and prosecute. This factor is increased if police forces are moving to a culture of decision-making that is "pro-charge" for acts of family violence. It is also easy to see the difficulties of investigating and prosecuting sexual crime, so the temptation, where violence is present, may be to lay charges for those actions only. Even when victims are asked about sexual abuses, and are prepared to detail them, investigator choices may be hampered by a victim's reluctance to sign statements, or want charges laid. There is not scope, within the parameters of this chapter, to do justice to the psychology of victim-survivors, when it comes to detailing the complexities of disclosure and reporting. For every complainant, the process will be unique, a combination of individual fears and anxieties, often accompanied by shame and self-blame, orchestrated by the offender, all the while wondering whether they will be listened to and believed, or judged and pilloried. What can be said here, however, is that all disclosure and reporting is a process which, when met with the right context, good communication skills, patience, and knowledge of offender behaviour and ensuing trauma, can lead to much better outcomes, whether forensic or therapeutic.

Secondly, the challenges of interviewing in relationship crime lead us to the next significant difference that, unlike sexual offending, family violence is usually responded to by *uniform members*, rather than detectives. Not only do most cases of family violence not require a specialist investigative response, but the sheer volume of reports means that responding will remain a generalist domain. In relation to risk assessment and interviewing, the more functional style of questioning necessary in general policing, particularly under the crisis conditions present when assessments and interviews are conducted, will predominate. The core skills of interviewing, building rapport, and listening are under severe pressure in these circumstances, demanding skill, and tact, to administer. Interviews need to be highly structured, and questioner-led, practises antithetical to the broader information-gathering style required of forensic investigations. In many ways, the questioner-led interviewing style required in family violence situations is sufficient to determine what immediate steps should be taken in relation to decisions regarding safety, or accessing services, but it will inevitably fall short of the standard required for forensic investigation of relationship crime. What is evident from research into reporting, trauma, and victim-centric practise is that, if victims are to detail the depth and breadth of the abuses perpetrated against them, every step of the process must be thought through. The ease of reporting, the context in which interviews take place, the processes followed, and the skills of the interviewer all require specialised processes and facilities, as well as specialised training and ongoing maintenance and development of interviewers' abilities. This is most true when it comes to interviewing children, and investigators are interested in interviewing children in these crime themes more than anywhere else. Specialised training in sexual crime investigation teaches that disclosure and reporting are a process, not a singular event. Investigators must be aware of the impacts of trauma on complainants and centre victims' needs in all interactions. They must not fall prey to any myths and misconceptions, particularly those concerning victim presentation during reports. They must not be confused by the fragmented nature of traumatised memories, and their interviewing technique must be skilled enough to elicit a complete, consistent, and coherent narrative, without altering it in any way. Finally, in a phase that may test the rapport they have assiduously built with the complainant, they must address any of her actions that fact finders may find hard to understand (as we do not yet teach jurors the basics of myth and misconception), to limit the damage defence counsel may later do in court. It should be abundantly clear, from this brief description, that forensic interviewing is a highly complex skill set, and difficult to master. The resources required to develop and run training, and maintain the skills to provide quality assurance, mean that it will remain outside the budgetary and rostering capability of police forces to provide such training for all police.

The third major difference concerns the mindset of attending members. Currently, those investigating sexual offending have an almost exclusively forensic focus. The only current exception to this, at least here in Victoria, occurs when the alleged offender is under the age of 18, where police may consider a therapeutic treatment order referral, rather than pursuing matters through the courts. This role may expand in future, should restorative justice initiatives roll out in different jurisdictions, or diversionary processes like Stop It Now receive approval to practise. Until then, the focus remains forensic, whereas family violence responders are immediately conscious of the potential for multiple pathways in any potential response to reports of family violence. These pathways entail three key elements: risk assessment, possible referral to a range of support services for victims of family violence, including some for perpetrators, as well as forensic options. When it comes to immediate responses, one can regularly hear the view that the culture of policing is shifting, in relation to forensic options for family violence, and is now "pro charge," demonstrating an increasing confidence not only in the backing of authorising officers within police, but in the wider court system. In sexual crime cases, although the options are purely forensic, it is harder to define where the culture currently sits. Despite significant advances in police practice, and much higher levels of community reporting, case attrition remains high, and conviction rates low, leaving lingering cynicism about the ease at which charges can be defended in adversarial courts. Research suggests these fears are well-founded, and that little has changed in the tactics employed by defence barristers over the years (Zydervelt et al. 2017). Attacking the credibility of the complainant is still the go-to strategy, rather than attacking the credibility of the complaint itself, often relying on myth and misconception to do so. In demonstrating that community attitudes are shifting, however, the same research found that, although prompting jurors to believe myths and misconceptions was a central tactic, defence counsel have a smaller arsenal to employ, as community awareness of the realities of sexual crime grows.

Lastly, in responding to family violence, police have multiple options in responding, including orders that keep perpetrators out-of-home or prohibit contact between perpetrator and victims, although orders are named differently across jurisdictions. In investigating sexual crime, the first response a suspect may perceive will come when he is interviewed and/or arrested, as confidentiality and secrecy are watchwords of sexual crime investigation. Incidentally, these differences of responses to victims are replicated across the wider community. For example, many jurisdictions now allow for leave and monetary support for victims of family violence, which represent a significant advance. No such architecture supports sexual crime victims. Even where community supports nominate sexual crime victims as potential users of their service, such as the national helpline (1800 Respect), family violence is seen as the dominant presenting issue, with no specialist counsellors available for callers about sexual offending, nor any ongoing specialist training in responding to victims of sexual crime for the counsellors.

The major risk in all of this, of course, is that the dominance of family violence responses, coupled with the assumption that most sexual offending is a subset of family violence, will lead to a gradual erosion of services to victims of sexual crime, and the significant advances made in this area, in the development of investigative methodology and forensic interviewing of both adults and children. On the other hand, there remains enormous potential to develop relationship-based crime investigation specialists, with knowledge and skills matched to both crime themes, that may further develop a specialist service. What should investigators do next in these scenarios, for example?

Case example 1

When attending a family violence incident, uniform officers asked the risk assessment question about sexual assault. The affected family member lowered her eyes and became silent. She did not answer, but took some time to compose herself before saying, "next question."

Case example 2

When attending a family violence incident, investigators note that the affected family member details violence towards herself and her three children. She also details repeated sexual assaults of her.

The case for specialism

Despite the differences in responding to family violence and sexual offending, notably in which police member attends the incident and what their priority pathways are, the similarities in both crime themes are overwhelming. Furthermore, training specialist investigators and providing them with bespoke conceptual approaches focusing on relationship evidence is considered to produce better outcomes (Darwinkel, Powell, & Tidmarsh 2013). Most important amongst them have been the increased satisfaction levels felt by complainants, a key element in recent rises in reporting rates.

So, is there a case for creating relationship-based crime commands in police services, and developing specialist investigators who can respond to both sexual offending and family violence matters? The move has already begun, although in fragmented ways. Victoria Police, for example, was the first service to create a Family Violence Command, designed to improve responses for uniform members, and create resources for the developing workforce of family violence investigators.

Subsumed within the Command sits the Sexual Offence and Child Abuse Team, servicing a highly developed workforce of specialist sexual offence and child abuse investigators, focused almost exclusively on forensic investigations, and with 12 years of experience with the new model. Whilst no policy of integration and overall specialism yet exists, members are already training together, and routinely working in each other's units, including authorising officers. Investigators describe the process of working across crime themes as "like switching heads," by which they mean an adjustment of procedural, safety planning, and investigative priorities. Although the switch may seem straightforward, experience in both sexual offence and family violence investigation is required to ensure investigators can do so effectively. If anyone is wondering why police services do not just throw them all together now, it is important to remember that focus on sexual offending is relatively recent, and police cultures and practises are notoriously slow to change. This has come about for many reasons, including a domination of focus on volume crime, over-valuing experience over innovation, and using investigators to be educators in all training programmes, rather than developing training alongside external expertise. Some police services around the world, desperate to speed up the process of change have adopted radical methods, like women-led police stations in Argentina (Carrington et al. 2020), a measure designed to overcome the problem of reporting by reducing fear and anxiety, and a familiar long-standing problem with sceptical male police officers, to reduce endemic problems of relationship violence.

However, should one follow the principle of integration, what implications might it have for recruitment, training, resourcing, continuous development, investigators' mental health, and improvements to investigative practise and case outcomes? Current models typically train all police officers to an initial standard, although some allow fast-track systems for those wishing to specialise as detectives, and both have their advantages and drawbacks. Critics of the latter suggest essential experience is missed, but critics of the former, and more relevant to these discussions, suggest that developing a one-size-fits-all approach disproportionately affects the more complex crime themes of sexual offending and family violence. Research we conducted looked at the skills and qualities most valued by investigators specialising in sexual offence and child abuse allegations and found five core qualities: empathy, good communication skills, patience, good investigative skills, and open-mindedness (Tidmarsh, Sharman, & Hamilton 2021). One could argue that these skills and qualities would improve all policing, but their absence has proved critical in the history of policing sexual offending and family violence. These skills and qualities also support the core skills of relationship-based crime investigation, namely listening, and interviewing. Police services who teach succinct, questioner-led interview styles, to all recruits, leave a legacy for all those who wish to move into relationship-based crime investigation. Such initial training leaves a template, demanding investigators wishing to move to narrative interview styles effectively de-train and re-train into the complainant-led, information-gathering process, more suited to relationship-based crime investigation. Gathering the "Whole Story," for example, is not possible without methodology that elicits depth and breadth in complainant narratives.

There has also been argument about how long investigators should remain in crime investigation areas that are emotionally and psychologically challenging, particularly where empathy is required. Empathy, whilst essential to good practice, also opens a window to trauma that can be hard to manage, often exacerbated by regularly witnessing victims' high levels of distress, or confronting the brutal realities of child exploitation material, for example. Some insist on time limits and rotation, but knowledge and subject matter expertise are hard won in these complex crime themes, so turnover carries significant risk. There is debate about how long investigators can remain in position without significant cost to themselves. Whilst it may seem logical that the rigours of the role will necessitate a time limit, it may also be argued that self-protection can be learned with experience. This is even more likely if they have regular access to mental health services. Victoria Police Family Violence Command, after much lobbying, introduced a Specialist Investigator Support Unit, to provide on-site group and individual supervision and therapeutic support, a move which has shown considerable benefits for staff, and protection against burn-out and mental health claims for those managing budgets.

Improvements to investigating sexual offending and family violence also carry an additional risk, for senior officers considering relationship-based crime specialism, because it will inevitably mean more investigations progress, and therefore more work. Those familiar with the tasks and processes of these complex investigations might then describe a workforce that knows what questions to ask, understands the disclosure and reporting process, knows how to build rapport, and to conduct thorough investigations. If investigators possess these skills and qualities, both sexual crime and family violence victims would be much more likely to move from "I'm not sure I want you to do anything about it," to "where do I sign?"

In all these practical considerations, two things are abundantly clear: that sexual offending and family violence require victim-centric and trauma-informed policing. Relationship-based crime investigation also requires specialist skills, qualities, and fit-for-purpose investigative methodologies that are beyond the scope of general policing. When members do encounter victim narratives, initial conversations or family violence risk assessment should be able to disseminate who requires the services of specialist investigation teams. Once they are there, irrespective of what report prompted the investigation, training, and protocol should help any investigator develop a narrative that captures the breadth and depth of the entire abusive relationship, including grooming and coercive control, as well as all violent and sexual abusive acts. Crucially, they must be able to find, where present, the damage done to children in these relationships, whether recognition of harms to them are present in the initial report or not.

From a specialist investigator point of view, the skills and qualities required to work in these crime themes are not present in every police officer, and that imagining the police service of the future may require radical changes to current protocols and paradigms. Is it time for fast-track into relationship-based crime investigation, specialist interviewers, career-long learning (particularly interviewing), and specialised mental health support that supports individuals and helps services maintain a healthy workforce?

Investigative challenges: "Whole Story" methodology

In the sphere of sexual offence investigation, traditional models of enquiry were focused on proof that offending "acts" had taken place, and detailing when and where events had occurred, which process is known as "particularisation'" (Powell, Roberts, & Guadagno 2007). Courts will always require particularisation to determine a finding of guilt for the act/s an offender is charged with. However, sexual offending is often a crime in and of relationship, whether familial or not, and explanations for what took place often occur before, during, and after the acts themselves, in the context of that relationship. To help investigators understand the dynamics of relationship-based crime, focus on the actions of the offender, particularly grooming, we developed investigative methodology that was a better fit for investigating sexual crime, which we describe as Whole Story investigation. It has had a significant impact on the investigation of sexual crime, notably on investigator attitudes towards victims (Tidmarsh, Hamilton, & Sharman 2020). This has come about, in part, due to the focus on offender behaviour which, in turn, frequently provides explanation for victims' behaviour, so much of which has traditionally been described as "counter-intuitive" and the subject of many myths and misconceptions.

In brief, Whole Story asserts that sexual offending is often a crime in and of relationship, which relationships are initiated by offenders and where victims are forced to respond to the grooming mechanisms driving the abusive relationship. Rather than focusing exclusively on offending "acts" Whole Story places those particularised acts within the context of the wider relationship, arguing that relevant evidence is being generated from the moment of first interaction, and that much of what explains subsequent actions, particularly victims' behaviour, occurs around the acts themselves. Most critically, evidence of grooming that established power and control, before chargeable acts have even occurred, may hold the keys to fact finders' understanding what has taken place. Most sexual offenders follow well-worn patterns of abusive behaviour, but they all do so with minor variations. As research demonstrates that fact finders can move beyond social and sexual scripts when presented with information in a novel way (Alison et al. 2012), and that the most persuasive aspects of any narrative are the "qualitative elements," Whole Story teaches investigators to prompt complainants' recall of "unique signifiers," as part of a complete, consistent, and coherent elicitation of each complainant's recollection of the offending relationship. This assists in determining appropriate avenues of enquiry, such as witnesses to the grooming. Focus on grooming and unique signifiers also improves the quality of suspect interview planning and, alongside appropriate interview protocols, in interviews themselves. The last two areas where

Whole Story has made a difference is in the quality of briefs presented, with potential benefits for increased authorisation, and in what prosecutors' call "case concept," the vital structure for how they will present the complainant's narrative to any fact finder or jury.

As yet, there is no Whole Story concept for family violence investigation, although there is considerable overlap. Family violence is understood in relationship, and the mechanisms of coercive control and grooming are, as we have argued, related as well as distinct. Furthermore, investigators have often, like the wider community, lacked understanding of the dynamics of abusive relationships and have fallen for misunderstandings and misconceptions, usually those that are critical of victim behaviour. For example, investigators have always been sceptical of complainants who withdrew their complaint, particularly when returning to relationships they had described as abusive. When attending incidents and being confronted by victims in a heightened state of emotion, investigators may also fall for the suspect's argument that she was just "hysterical," a word that would resonate with anyone understanding the origins of understanding child sexual abuse. The strongest difference in eliciting the Whole Story, in sexual or family violence investigations may come, not in the conceptual framework and investigative structure, but in questions of who would elicit the complainant narrative, when they might do so, and with what endgame in mind. In short, who would conduct the interview, with what methodology, and to what purpose?

Interviewing, authorising briefs, and prosecuting

As we have discussed previously, in this chapter, forensic interviewing, in the information-gathering style, remains the core skill set of any relationship-based crime investigator. In family violence cases, however, it may be far less critical to case outcomes than with sexual offence investigations. Not only might the outcome of any interview not lead to charges that proceed to court, but even if it does, evidence may be more visible and readily understandable than in sexual offences. In understanding sexual crime, where witnesses to the acts themselves are few and far between the narrative, and therefore the interviewing, is everything. It is also that narrative, in sexual crime cases, that heralds the beginning of the investigation. Family violence investigations may begin with only a cursory round up of relevant facts. When investigators come with a variety of intentions and outcomes, relatively little evidence may be needed to ascertain what outcomes can be put in place. In sexual crime investigation, evidence must be elicited for the entirety of the abusive relationship, in as much breadth and depth as possible.

The primary purpose of interviewing, in this forensic environment, is to elicit evidence that may be presented to a magistrate or jury, depending on the severity of the behaviour and nature of the charge. The historical problem has been, for a variety of reasons, that there are many barriers to overcome before cases are heard in courts. We have already spoken about low reporting and case attrition, most of which takes place in the early stages of investigation, but let us now turn to the critical point in the downstream orientation phenomenon, when authorising officers consider a brief of evidence and whether the narrative they are presenting will provide "a reasonable prospect of conviction" (OPP 2022). At this juncture, both sexual offending and family violence cases have often foundered, particularly in sexual crime investigations. The biggest hurdle remains that relatively few victims report abuses, despite significant increases in recent years. The next is where decisions are made about what can be heard, and understood, by fact finders. The two points, obviously, are intrinsically linked, as they concern public attitudes and beliefs, social and sexual scripts, and the phenomena of judgment and doubt. In deciding whether to report, victims typically fear judgement, doubt, and disbelief from those they report to. At the point of authorisation, professionals fear the prospect, particularly where 12 members of the public must reach unanimous conclusions, of eliminating any, and all, doubt. As there are no guides to how one might determine "a reasonable prospect," decisions are made around the other vague terms of common sense, or experience. What this has meant, in practice, with court officials' awareness of the plethora of myths and misconceptions about sexual offending and family violence held by fact finders, is that many deserving narratives are never heard. In many jurisdictions, victims also have a hard time appealing decisions once authorising police officers, or prosecutors, have decided their narrative has not met the threshold.

Even where the narratives are compelling, cases may be turned down because of issues related to another vague term, "credibility" (ALRC 2010). Defence counsel's main role remains, across both these crime themes, to diminish the credibility of the complainant, rather than the credibility of the complaint itself. Of the many reasons this is still their most effective strategy, there are three we would like to concentrate on here. Firstly, in relationship-based crime, victims are the sole witness to the abusive acts. As we have seen, traditional investigative models did little to counter this, ignoring the breadth and depth of understandings emanating from witnesses to the entire relationship. So, if they could damage the only "witness," their job was done. Secondly, attacking victims' credibility was made easy by the breadth of community myth and misconception, often facilitated by other "non-judicial" credibility factors (O'Neal, Tellis, & Spohn 2015). To name a few, from a depressingly long list: victims' sexual history could be brought up, irrespective to its relevance in the matter at hand, children's memories were regarded as unreliable, despite research to the contrary, and both sexual offence and family violence victims would routinely have matters of mental health records raised, irrespective of their relevance to the alleged offences. Whilst rules have tightened, most of these tactics remain in play (Zyderveldt et al. 2017).

Thirdly, of note in sexual crime cases, the law often offers a double chance for accused persons in matters of consent (Fileborn 2011). Most jurisdictions in Australia, and across the world, when it has been established that the victim in question was not consenting, still allow the argument that the accused person had formed a "reasonable belief" that she was. All this has been made easier for accused persons by the inadequacy of traditional investigative techniques, missing the grooming and coercive control of perpetrators, and concentrating only on chargeable acts. In family violence cases, for example, we have also allowed defences of provocation, or that offenders "snapped" in momentary losses of control. In abuses against LGBTQIA+ victims we have allowed the absurd defence of "gay panic" (Equality Australia 2020), drawing on homophobic attitudes to licence violence. In all these decisions, and the fundamental assumption that "reason" is fair and unbiased, there is a backdrop of patriarchy, misogyny, and prejudice, brought about by dominance of law and policing by men. Many changes have been made, but progress has been slow. Furthermore, as the science refuting myths and misconceptions becomes ever more compelling, there are no requirements, in many jurisdictions, for jurors to be informed about it. Trials have shown that non-case-specific training of potential jurors can have a significant impact on the number of myths and misconceptions prompted by defence (Blackwell 2008; Blackwell & Seymour 2014). Court officials too, for the most part, are under no requirement to educate themselves about criminological or forensic psychological advances. Perhaps it is felt that the law will suffice in providing direction, as it is in courts where appeals are heard, where judges need not even have criminal law experience, never mind experience of sexual offending and family violence cases.

How would prosecutors deal with these scenarios, for example?

Case example 3

When attending a family violence incident, investigators gather a wealth of evidence, including photographs of injuries and witnesses to multiple acts of violence. The premises also bear the marks of violence detailed in statements, including holes in walls, broken furniture, and a collection of knives. The affected family member also details a litany of rapes and sexual assaults, interspersed in a sexual relationship she describes as "mostly consensual." Investigators consider what charges they will lay, if any, of rape or sexual assault.

Case example 4

Specialist sexual crime investigators take a statement from a complainant of multiple rapes and sexual assaults by her partner, including video recordings and photographs. They are confident of laying several charges, all carrying significant potential penalties. She also catalogues a long history of coercive control, physical assaults, which they believe will make authorisation of a brief of evidence straightforward. They consider whether to lay charges for the physical assaults which, unusually, has less compelling evidence to support it, and carries significantly lesser penalties.

Conclusion

The policing of sexual crime and family violence, after a long and dispiriting history of failure, and profoundly un-victim-centric practice, is finally coming of age.

Unparalleled research focus and developing public awareness have created calls for change that are being heeded by policymakers and frontline members alike. There remain significant challenges, however, if responses to both sexual offending and family violence are going to be effective. Chief among those challenges may be understandings of how, and where, they intersect. Core elements, of grooming and coercive control, of the predominance of abuse in relationship, all suggest that similarities outweigh differences. However, such differences as there are, of victim experience, offender psychology, methodology and intent, and of policing requirements, suggest much more thought must go into developing relationship-crime investigations and responses. Core of any thinking should be an understanding of unique victim experiences and needs, and the need to develop victim-centric responses. In the future, perhaps most police forces will have relationship-based crime commands, with agendas driven by research and practise analysis, effortlessly managing the gargantuan task of addressing sexual offending and family violence and maintaining specialist responses for the unique elements of each crime.

Note

1 This is an extrapolation from three different sets of statistics. Whilst reporting figures may vary, most suggest that approximately one in eight adults report sexual crime (Home Office 2011), and approximately one in ten children (London et al. 2008; Radford et al. 2011), but only about one-third of reporters do so within 72 hours of the offence. Seventy-two hours is a common timeframe for designating an "immediate" report (again, this figure may vary). Subsequently, the figure for overall "immediate" reporting is about 5%. Even if rates change at different times, and statistics vary, it demonstrates that delayed reporting is far more common than immediate reporting, and not "counter-intuitive" at all.

References

AIHW, 2019. *Family, domestic and sexual violence in Australia 2018*. Australian Institute of Health & Welfare, Canberra.

Alison, L., Almond, L., Christiansen, P., Waring, S., Power, N., and Villejoubert, G., 2012. When do we believe experts? The power of the unorthodox view. *Behavioral Sciences & the Law*, *30*(6), pp. 729–748.doi: 10.1002/bsl.2030

ALRC, 2010. *Uniform evidence law (ALRC Report 102): 18. Comments, warnings and directions to the jury*. Australian Law Reform Commission, Canberra.

Bagwell-Gray, M.E., Messing, J.T., and Baldwin-White, A., 2015. Intimate partner sexual violence: A review of terms, definitions, and prevalence. *Trauma, Violence, & Abuse*, *16*(3), pp. 316–335. doi:10.1177/1524838014557290

Bidarra, Z.S., Lessard, G., and Dumont, A., 2016. Co-occurrence of intimate partner violence and child sexual abuse: Prevalence, risk factors and related issues. *Child Abuse & Neglect*, *55*, pp. 10–21. doi:10.1016/j.chiabu.2016.03.007

Blackwell, S., 2008, 'Child sexual abuse on trial in New Zealand', paper presented at the *New Zealand Law Foundation Intensive Criminal Law Symposium*, Auckland, November 2008.

Blackwell, S. and Seymour, F., 2014. Prediction of jury verdicts in child sexual assault trials. *Psychiatry, Psychology and Law*, *21*(4), pp. 567–576. doi:10.1080/13218719.2013.856278

Bright, S., Roach, C., Barnaba, L., Walker, S., and Millsteed, M., 2021. *Attrition of sexual offence incidents through the Victorian criminal justice system: 2021 update*. Crime Statistics Agency, Melbourne.

Campbell, J.C., Webster, D., Koziol-McLain, J., Block, C., Campbell, D., Curry, M.A., Gary, F., Glass, N., McFarlane, J., Sachs, C., and Sharps, P., 2003. Risk factors for femicide in abusive relationships: Results from a multisite case control study. *American Journal of Public Health, 93*(7), pp.1089–1097. doi:10.2105/AJPH.93.7.1089

Carrington, K., Guala, N., Puyol, M.V., and Sozzo, M., 2020. How women's police stations empower women, widen access to justice and prevent gender violence. *International Journal for Crime, Justice and Social Democracy, 9*(1), pp. 42–67. doi:10.5204/ijcjsd.v9i1.1494

Daly, K. and Bouhours, B., 2010. Rape and attrition in the legal process: A comparative analysis of five countries. *Crime and Justice, 39*(1), pp. 565–650. doi:10.1086/653101

Darwinkel, E., Powell, M., and Tidmarsh, P., 2013. Prosecutors' perceptions of the utility of 'relationship' evidence in sexual abuse trials. *Australian & New Zealand Journal of Criminology, 47*(1), pp. 44–58. doi:10.1177/0004865813497733

Equality Australia, 2020. *'Gay panic' defence to murder abolished Australia-wide*. Australia.

Fileborn, B., 2011. *Sexual assault laws in Australia*. Australian Institute of Family Studies, Melbourne.

Home Office, 2011. *The stern review: Treatment of rape complaints*. Government Equalities Office, London.

London, K., Bruck, M., Wright, D.B., and Ceci, S.J., 2008. Review of the contemporary literature on how children report sexual abuse to others: Findings, methodological issues, and implications for forensic interviewers. *Memory, 16*(1), pp. 29–47. doi:10.1080/09658210701725732

Martin, S.L., Ray, N., Sotres-Alvarez, D., Kupper, L.L., Moracco, K.E., Dickens, P.A., Scandlin, D., and Gizlice, Z., 2006. Physical and sexual assault of women with disabilities. *Violence against Women, 12*(9), pp. 823–837. doi:10.1177/1077801206292672

MoJ, 2013. *Statistics on race and the criminal justice system 2012*. Ministry of Justice, London.

Murray, S. and Heenan, M., 2012. Reported rapes in Victoria: Police responses to victims with a psychiatric disability or mental health issue. *Current Issues in Criminal Justice, 23*(3), pp. 353–368. doi:10.1080/10345329.2012.12035929

Murray, S. and Powell, A., 2008. *Sexual assaults and adults with a disability: Enabling recognition, disclosure, and a just response*. Australian Institute of Family Studies, Melbourne.

O'Neal, E.N., Tellis, K., and Spohn, C., 2015. Prosecuting intimate partner sexual assault: Legal and extra-legal factors that influence charging decisions. *Violence against Women, 21*(10), pp. 1237–1258. doi:10.1177/1077801215591630

OPP, 2022. *Policy of the director of public prosecutions for Victoria*. Office of Public Prosecutions, Victoria.

Pattavina, A., Morabito, M., and Williams, L.M., 2016. Examining connections between the police and prosecution in sexual assault case processing: Does the use of exceptional clearance facilitate a downstream orientation?. *Victims & Offenders, 11*(2), pp. 315–334. doi:10.1080/15564886.2015.1046622

Powell, M., Roberts, K., and Guadagno, B., 2007. Particularisation of child abuse offences: Common problems when questioning child witnesses. *Current Issues in Criminal Justice, 19*(1), pp. 64–74. doi:10.1080/10345329.2007.12036415

Radford, L., Corral, S., Bradley, C., Fisher, H., Bassett, C., Howat, N., and Collishaw, S., 2011. *Child Abuse and Neglect in the UK Today*. NSPCC, London.

Rich, K. and Seffrin, P., 2014. Birds of a feather or fish out of water? Policewomen taking rape reports. *Feminist Criminology, 9*(2), pp. 137–159. doi:1557085113510551

Rothman, E.F., Exner, D., and Baughman, A.L., 2011. The prevalence of sexual assault against people who identify as gay, lesbian, or bisexual in the United States: A systematic review. *Trauma, Violence, & Abuse, 12*(2), pp. 55–66. doi:10.1177/1524838010390707

SSCRFV, 2006. *Reforming the family violence system in Victoria*. Statewide Steering Committee to Reduce Family Violence, Office of Women's Policy, Melbourne.

SSCRSA, 2006. *Study of reported rapes in Victoria 2000–2003*. Statewide Steering Committee to Reduce Sexual Assault, Office of Women's Policy, Melbourne.

Tidmarsh, P., Hamilton, G., and Sharman, S.J., 2020. Changing police officers' attitudes in sexual offense cases: A 12-month follow-up study. *Criminal Justice and Behavior, 47*(9), pp. 1176–1189. doi:10.1177/0093854820921201

Tidmarsh, P., Sharman, S., and Hamilton, G., 2021. Police officers' perceptions of specialist training, skills and qualities needed to investigate sexual crime. *Police Practice and Research, 22*(1), pp. 475–490. doi:10.1080/15614263.2019.1697266

VHREOC, 2015. *Independent review into sex discrimination and sexual harassment, including predatory behaviour, in Victoria Police: Phase 1 Report*. Victorian Human Rights and Equal Opportunity Commission, Melbourne.

Victorian Government, 2016. *Royal Commission into family violence: Summary and recommendations*. RCFV, Victoria.

VLRC, 2004. *Sexual offences report*. Victorian Law Reform Commission, Melbourne.

VSA, 2015. *Annual Report 2015*. Victim Support Agency, Melbourne.

Walters, M., Chen, J., and Breiding, M., 2011. *National intimate partner and sexual violence survey 2010: Findings on victimization by sexual orientation*. Center for Victim Research, Washington.

WHO, 2002. *World report on violence and health*. Word Health Organisation, Geneva.

Zydervelt, S., Zajac, R., Kaladelfos, A., and Westera, N., 2017. Lawyers' strategies for cross-examining rape complainants: Have we moved beyond the 1950s?. *British Journal of Criminology, 57*(3), pp. 551–569. doi:10.1093/bjc/azw023

5

CHILDREN, FAMILY VIOLENCE, AND SEXUAL ABUSE

The undetected victims?

Children have traditionally been hidden victims of violence, both within and outside of family contexts. Some progress in recognising children as victims has been made over time. Three decades ago, many countries became signatories to the United Nations Convention on the Rights of the Child, an international commitment to preserve and promote the rights of children. In particular, Article 19 articulates that governments should protect children from violence, abuse, and neglect by parents and caregivers, and Article 34 extends this to include a protection from sexual abuse. In Australia, for example, the federal government invested half a billion dollars into the 2013 Royal Commission into Institutional Responses to Child Sexual Abuse—one of the largest public inquiries internationally. The Royal Commission shed light on historical cases of child sexual abuse and how institutions addressed allegations, resulting in over 100 recommendations for organisations and governments to try to correct past wrongdoings and improve future responses.

While such progress is promising, children continue to be overlooked, or thought of as simply extensions of their parents' experiences (Meyer 2020). Worst still, the lockdowns arising from the global COVID-19 pandemic have exacerbated the conditions for child abuse to breed and have rendered children even more invisible than before. Donagh (2020), an operations manager of two specialist children's services in the United Kingdom, reflects that there has been an increase in reports to domestic violence services from adult victims, yet the same increases have not been seen with children and young people. A key reason is the closure of schools, youth clubs, and sporting clubs—safe havens for children to escape abuse at home and disclose abuse to trusted adults outside of the family. As Donagh details, schools are one of the main referral pathways to domestic violence and abuse services, so their closure makes it difficult to identify abuse in a cohort who were already going unnoticed prior to lockdowns. Some research also indicates that lockdowns have increased rates of online child sexual abuse and exploitation; the National Crime

DOI: 10.4324/9781003051657-6

Agency (2020) warned that the numbers of U.K. people who posed a sexual threat to children doubled since the year prior to the pandemic unfolding, from 140,000 to 300,000.

Chapter 5 will begin with an overview of the semantics and definitions used to denote children who are exposed to or involved in family violence. It will then provide a synthesis of empirical literature on the links between intimate partner violence and child abuse (with a focus on sexual violence), followed by a consideration of the relationships between intimate partner violence, sibling abuse, and child-to-parent abuse. Finally, this chapter will turn to a commentary on the different services and systems that impact children experiencing family violence, and the need to integrate and/or build capacity of services to better meet the needs of children, particularly those who are at risk of or who have experienced child sexual abuse.

Definitions that distance and discern children

While definitions of family and sexual violence (including child sexual abuse) were discussed in Chapter 1, it is important to further delve into the language used to describe children who are exposed to and involved in domestic and family violence. Historically, language used to describe children in domestic violence situations has often distanced children from their experiences. For example, children have been described as mere witnesses to intimate partner violence or "unintended victims" who may be considered collateral damage or caught in the crossfire (Goddard & Bedi 2010). Yet such language may be inaccurate and only serve to minimise children's traumatic experiences. These terminological weaknesses prompted Goddard and Bedi to adopt the term "children forced to live with intimate partner violence" as they rationalised it identifies the problem with specificity but encompasses the many ways that children may experience family violence, while also emphasising their lack of choice and autonomy. In their explanation, they also acknowledge that children can simultaneously experience harm from exposure to intimate partner violence, while also being the direct targets of abuse (e.g., through physical and sexual abuse).

Extant police cases demonstrate how children can be the target victims of abuse, even when cases present as violence between intimate partners. As discussed in Chapter 1, intimate partner violence may be instrumental in grooming child victims into sexual abuse (e.g., the violence towards mother is signalling the perpetrator's power and sending a message to the daughter to comply). The perpetrator may be using the intimate partner as a means to an end, where the ultimate goal is to sexually abuse the child. Our interviewees also described cases to us where mothers were raped because they were protecting their daughters from sexual harm. Such cases highlight the complexities of family violence and the need to consider cases from multiple perspectives, including child-centred and sexual abuse perspectives, so that child victims do not fall through the cracks.

In terms of legislative definitions, children's exposure to and involvement in family violence is now recognised as a harm in many jurisdictions. For example, in

England, Northern Ireland, and Wales, the definition of harm to children includes "impairment suffered from seeing or hearing the ill-treatment of another" (Section 120, *Adoption and Children Act 2002*; *Family Homes and Domestic Violence (Northern Ireland) Order 1998*). More recently, the *Domestic Abuse Act 2021* in England recognises children as victims of domestic violence if they "see or hear, or experience the effects of the abuse," and where at least one party to the domestic abuse is related to or has parental responsibility of the child. This legislation is mirrored in Australia (*Family Law Act 1975 (Cth)*), with several examples of what constitutes children being exposed to violence:

- Overhearing threats of death or injury by a family member towards another family member.
- Seeing or hearing an assault of a family member by another family member.
- Providing comfort or assistance to a family member where they have been assaulted by another family member.
- Cleaning up a site after a family member has intentionally damaged property of another family member.
- Being present when police or ambulance officers attend an incident involving the assault of a family member by another family member.

In Scotland, domestic abuse is now legally recognised as a form of child abuse (Section 24, *Family Law (Scotland) Act, 2006*). It is also considered an aggravated offence if the domestic abuse directly or indirectly involves children (*Domestic Abuse (Scotland) Act 2018*).

Conceptualisations and definitions of domestic violence across the globe are increasingly recognising coercive controlling behaviours (e.g., emotional and financial abuse, isolation, and monitoring), however, some scholars have pointed out that children are overlooked in these understandings (Katz 2016; Katz, Nikupeteri, & Laitinen 2020). Katz (2016) highlighted that we have tended to adopt a physical incident model regarding children's experiences of domestic abuse, whereby we think of the harms towards children as discrete incidents of physical abuse. On the contrary, we now know that children also experience the harms of coercive control. Indeed, interviews with mothers and children (aged 10–14 years) from the United Kingdom have indicated that children suffer a range of non-physically abusive behaviours that are inherent to coercive control (Katz 2016). Examples include abusive fathers preventing children from spending time with other people such as mothers, grandparents, and friends, and restricting their participation in extracurricular activities. This excessive control over children's lives leaves them feeling isolated and disempowered, with lack of opportunities to develop loving connections, social skills, confidence, and resilience.

Research also indicates that children experience enduring harm from coercive control even after parents have separated. For example, a study with young people in the United Kingdom and Finland (aged 4–21 years old) found that many children viewed their abusive fathers as a mentally omnipresent figure, even after they discontinued contact (Katz, Nikupeteri, & Laitinen 2020). This had a significant impact on children's psychological well-being, with accounts that they were constantly fearful, resulting in anxiety, panic attacks, bed-wetting, and nightmares. In order to escape their abusive father, some children relayed how they had to move houses several times. This continual uprooting meant that children often had to leave their schools and friends, which, in turn, impacted their relationships with peers and educational achievements. Based on these experiences, the authors have advocated for the use of a coercive control-based definition of domestic abuse in future domestic abuse work with children as opposed to the physical incident model. They also suggest the need for legislation to recognise children as victim-survivors of coercive control in their own right.

Associations between child abuse and intimate partner violence

Worldwide estimates of child abuse indicate that it is widespread, with approximately 1 billion children aged 2–17 years experiencing physical, sexual, or emotional violence and neglect in the year prior (Hillis et al. 2016). In the United States, for example, every nine minutes, child protective services find evidence for a claim of child sexual abuse, with 1 in 9 girls and 1 in 53 boys under the age of 18 experiencing sexual abuse by an adult (RAINN 2021). Due to the private and hidden nature of child abuse and barriers to reporting, such figures are also likely to be an underestimation.

After decades of research, the connection between child abuse and intimate partner violence is now well-established (Appel & Holden 1998; Bidarra, Lessard, & Dumont 2016; Hamby et al. 2010; Herrenkohl et al. 2008). While rates vary between different samples and locations, there is consensus that there is an overlapping relationship between intimate partner violence and child abuse. Firstly, research has revealed a significant link between intimate partner violence and child physical abuse. In a review of 31 empirical studies, mostly from the United States, a median co-occurrence rate of 40% was found (Appel & Holden 1998). Such an estimate may be conservative, however, as mothers were the sole informants of the co-occurrence rates in the majority of studies, and there may be a plethora of reasons why mothers may provide inaccurate reports of child abuse (e.g., fear of the perpetrator, fear of child removal from child protection services, unawareness of child abuse).

Research has also established a significant link between intimate partner violence and child sexual abuse (Bidarra et al. 2016; Goddard & Hiller 1993; Hamby et al. 2010). In a review of ten empirical studies (from the United States, Canada, the United Kingdom, and Colombia), co-occurrence rates varied from 12% to 70%, concluding that children who are exposed to intimate partner violence are at a greater risk of being victims of intrafamilial sexual abuse or other maltreatment (Bidarra et al. 2016). For example, an American study found that more than 70% of young people who reported being sexually abused by a known adult had also witnessed intimate partner violence between their parents or caregivers (Hamby et al. 2010). Interestingly, young people who reported witnessing intimate partner violence were also at an increased likelihood of entering problematic intimate relationships in their adolescence; lifetime reports indicated that 55.7% of dating violence victims and 52.6% of rape and sexual misconduct victims had a history of witnessing partner violence.

There is also considerable evidence that experiencing child sexual abuse is a risk factor for experiences of domestic abuse, including, but not limited to, intimate partner sexual violence, in adulthood (Daigneault, Hébert, & McDuff 2009; Fry, McCoy, & Swales 2012; Garcia-Linares et al. 2005; Jennings et al. 2015; Renner & Slack 2006). In a large Canadian study, women who reported child sexual abuse were 2.75 times more likely to experience physical violence, and 3.68 times more likely to experience sexual violence by a current or previous partner, compared to women who had not reported child sexual abuse (Daigneault et al. 2009). The increased likelihood was established, even after controlling for a host of socio-demographic variables.

Experiences of child sexual abuse are also associated with the perpetration of intimate partner violence in adulthood (Fang & Corso 2007; Jennings et al. 2015; Renner & Whitney 2012; Widom et al. 2014). In a study with American university students, individuals who had experienced child sexual abuse were nearly two times more likely to perpetrate physical violence in adult dating relationships compared to individuals who had not experienced child sexual abuse (Jennings et al. 2015). The findings remained significant, even when removing systematic differences between the two groups, suggesting a direct link between child sexual abuse and intimate partner violence perpetration. It is important to emphasise, however, that such findings should not be used to stigmatise victims of child sexual abuse. Most children who experience abuse will not become perpetrators, yet it is clear that this risk factor requires attention in prevention and intervention efforts. This point was summarised by one of our stakeholder interviewees:

> Although not all people who have experienced child abuse go on to be perpetrators, what we also know is that those in our prisons, that's something they share—a child abuse history. So in order to change it and stop, to create a community or world free from violence, we've got to pay attention to children. If we don't, we're going to keep reacting, so that's the importance of it.
>
> *Narelle Goodland, Principal Practitioner at a policing organisation*

This point has also been echoed by experts in family violence who have called for greater funding into primary prevention initiatives for children and young people to help reduce the intergenerational transmission of violence (Fitz-Gibbon & Meyer 2021). Indeed, researchers have identified a dearth of primary prevention programmes for young children, especially those aged eight years and under (Campo et al. 2014). It is now an unequivocal finding that children who are exposed to or involved in family violence are at a heightened risk of suffering from ongoing negative social, emotional, psychological, and health outcomes (e.g., depression, anxiety, aggression, low self-esteem, poor academic outcomes, impaired cognitive functioning; Campo et al. 2014). This finding, paired with the research above highlighting increased victimisation and perpetration trajectories, underlines the urgent need to focus on children in family violence and sexual abuse prevention efforts.

Sibling and child-to-parent abuse

Intimate partner violence can permeate throughout the home and influence children's use of violence, highlighting the complicated status of children as simultaneous victims and "perpetrators" of violence. Some research has indicated that abuse and conflict between spouses is associated with child abuse, which is, in turn, related to violence and conflict between siblings (Hoffman, Kiecolt, & Edwards 2005). The same study also found that witnessing parental arguments was associated with higher levels of sibling violence. Some of our stakeholder interviewees indicated how a violent home can create the perfect formula for child sexual abuse to flourish. For example, Team Leader at Kids First Australia, Shureeka Alves, explained how in some violent households, the child's needs are not being met by parents, so they look for love and connection in different relationships, sometimes with siblings. Children may seek emotional and physical intimacy with siblings, but the boundaries get blurred, especially during a child's sexual development. This notion is illustrated in the following hypothetical case study, based on de-identified information from our interviews:

> Cedric, a 9-year-old boy, is part of a family of four children. His mother and father have a long history of domestic abuse. Cedric and his three siblings have moved houses several times to flee their abusive father. They are currently living in a small rental house where he shares a bedroom with his older brother and two younger sisters. Cedric is used to huddling up in bed with his siblings while his parents are fighting. He has become very close with them and often shares a bed with them. Cedric has begun to notice his older brother watching movies on his phone with naked people in them. He feels embarrassed watching them but laughs with his brother. He doesn't really understand what's happening in the videos, but his brother shows him how to copy some of the actions.

This case study elucidates how certain habits (e.g., sleeping in the same bed, long periods without parental supervision) might form when violence flares up in a household, but it is difficult to undo those habits when violence has settled (if at all). In particular, it might be difficult to re-establish clear boundaries about privacy and appropriate behaviours between siblings. The case study also demonstrates how children may develop inappropriate coping mechanisms in order to regulate emotions, and problematic behaviours may go unnoticed by parents if they are pre-occupied with their own abuse and the potential aftermath of violence (e.g., moving houses). Our interview with Shureeka also re-iterated the need for responses to child sexual abuse to be multi-faceted and consider sexual abuse and family violence as interrelated as opposed to discrete experiences. Here she elaborates:

> If we think about repairing relationships, it's really difficult to do the sexual abuse work if you don't address the family violence. Because if we go straight into the sexual abuse stuff, sometimes I feel like that is a symptom of family violence, hence why we'll need to address that. It goes hand in hand – you can't do the sexual abuse work without addressing the family violence, it's like a band aid solution.
>
> *Shureeka Alves, Team Leader at Kids First Australia*

Research has also indicated that child abuse—both exposure to intimate partner violence and direct victimisation—are predictors of child-to-parent violence. For example, a meta-analysis of 19 empirical studies found that child victims of parent violence were approximately 70% more likely to exercise physical, psychological, and emotional abuse towards parents compared to children who had not experienced abuse by parents (Gallego et al. 2019). Parent abuse is typically defined as a pattern of behaviour that uses verbal, financial, physical, or emotional means to exert power and control over a parent (Holt 2012). Interviews with abused mothers have highlighted a range of common abusive behaviours such as the silent treatment, name calling, property damage, choking, threats to kill or sexually assault, and harming or killing the family pet (Stewart, Burns, & Leonard 2007). Such abuse can take a significant toll on family members, including damage to physical and mental health and economic hardship (Fitz-Gibbon, Elliott, & Maher 2018).

Police and other practitioners also need to be careful in their response to children and adolescents using violence in the home, as it may be indicative of their own abuse and trauma. Based on de-identified interview information, the following is a hypothetical case study of a young person using violence in the home:

> Frontline police have responded six separate times to calls of verbal and physical abuse towards a mother by her 12-year-old son, Tom. The mother reports that her son has punched a hole in the wall, pushed and slapped her resulting in a very bruised cheek, and yelled at her, calling her a "stupid slut who deserves to be raped." Police have issued Tom with intervention orders, where he has received warnings for breaches. They have also tried some community policing initiatives where they have visited Tom's football games in an attempt to build a positive and supportive relationship. The violent behaviour towards his mother, however, has persisted, leaving her feeling hopeless about her and Tom's future.

On the face of this case, Tom can be framed as a perpetrator of family violence. Yet with further probing and the adoption of a child-centred approach, it became apparent that Tom was suffering and acting out in response to his own abuse. Tom's behaviour was reportedly fine in the classroom at school, but at night he regularly escaped his room and slept on the roof. He also avoided the shower, indicating he did not feel safe in his bedroom or bathroom.

When police engaged specialist investigators from the sexual offences and child abuse team, it was confirmed that Tom was experiencing sexual abuse by another member of the family. This type of case is also in line with research that has found many children and adolescents who use violence in the home have witnessed violence or been physically and/or sexually abused (Cottrell & Monk 2004; Kennair & Mellor 2007), and/or have experienced trauma (Campbell et al. 2020). It is important to recognise, however, that there are multiple pathways to child-to-parent violence, and we must be careful not to dismiss all victims of parent abuse as perpetrators, as this will only serve to shame parents and create barriers to help-seeking.

The above case signals the need for therapeutic as opposed to criminal justice responses for young people who use violence in the home. It also demonstrates the complex nature of children as both users and subjects of violence, and the need for responders to have awareness about the interrelationships between domestic violence and child sexual abuse. As summarised by Principal Practitioner, Narelle Goodland:

> Bringing people together with different lenses is the only way we're going to truly be able to achieve what everyone wants to achieve... We're geared for victims and we're geared for perpetrators but we're not geared when you're both; its really hard for the criminal justice system to respond to the complex needs of children in those circumstances... We know it's the frontline police who are going to the majority of family violence incidents—they need tools and support to think about children to know the warning signs of potentially where sexual abuse might be brewing.

When planets collide: Systems and services that impact children

Scholars and policymakers have increasingly documented the disjointed nature of services for family violence cases that involve children (Campo et al. 2014). Indeed, Hester (2011) has described the tensions and contradictions between domestic violence, child protection, and child contact (family law) sectors as the "three planet model" because each sector has its own histories, cultures, and laws, and operates according to different assumptions and practises. The planets then "collide" when a child experiences domestic violence (Powell & Murray 2008), which may ultimately pose issues for women and children's welfare.

In short, the domestic violence sector has developed alongside women's movements and tends to recognise the gendered nature of abuse, where women are primarily the victim-survivors of men's violence and coercive controlling behaviours (Hester 2011). This sector's main focus is on adults who are voluntarily seeking help for violence. Children's needs may be treated as secondary to their mothers or addressed as an extension of their mother's needs. This approach was highlighted in one of our interviews with a family violence crisis worker:

> if a woman comes and seeks support whether that's through outreach or through basic family violence service, we will support the child indirectly… we would support them through the victim survivor herself… If a child victim-survivor comes to see us for support we would tell them to go to child protection.

This same theme is echoed in research with directors of domestic violence and sexual assault agencies in the United States; directors acknowledged the importance of children's services but stated funding limitations and the demands of serving adult victim-survivors were key barriers to offering specialised children's services (Macy et al. 2010).

Conversely, child protection's main focus is on children, where social worker's main aims are to ensure children are safe in their home, with the removal of children into state care as an option if children's welfare is at risk (Hester 2011). While the child protection sector prioritises the safety of children, this may come at the expense of abused mothers in domestic violence contexts. Researchers have pointed out that there is an expectation that mothers keep their children safe, and mothers experiencing domestic violence may be punished for remaining in a violent relationship, with the ultimate blow of having their children removed (Hester 2011; Humphreys 2008; Powell & Murray 2008). These fears and realities are amplified for many marginalised women, and in particular First Nations women, who have a long and fraught history with the forcible removal of their children by governments. For example, in Australia, a key barrier preventing Aboriginal and Torres Strait Islander women from reporting family violence is the concern that their children will be removed (Langton et al. 2020). This has prompted researchers and policymakers to reflect on the potential implications of co-locating child protection services with other domestic violence services in multi-disciplinary hubs for victim-survivors.

The third intersecting "planet" that is frequently involved in family violence cases involving children are the family law courts, which determine the custody of children when parents have separated (Hester 2011). It is now well established that family violence is prevalent in cases referred for child custody evaluation (e.g., Johnston et al. 2005), yet legal professionals (e.g., judges, attorneys, custody evaluators) continue to overestimate the rate of false allegations of family violence and minimise or ignore reports of domestic violence in their decision-making (Saunders, Faller, & Tolman 2012). For example, victim-survivors of domestic abuse in the United States have reported feeling defeated in child custody hearings because their reports of abuse were met with disbelief and hostility. Reports of abuse were misrepresented, or in some cases deemed irrelevant and excluded altogether from custody evaluator's reports (Saunders et al. 2012). In particular, when mothers tried to alert the family law system about their children's abuse, they were viewed as deceptive and punished with restricted access to their children. In the same study, a questionnaire of U.S. professionals involved in child custody cases revealed several important findings: a lack of knowledge about family violence, negative views about victims of family violence (e.g., domestic violence victims alienate children from their other parent), and a belief that family violence is not an important factor in custody decisions. A lack of knowledge and negative beliefs about victims were also positively related to professionals' custody recommendations that favoured perpetrators (e.g., unsupervised visitation, joint and, in some cases, sole custody).

The underlying philosophy of the family law system is that families should be preserved and that children should have contact with both parents (Hester 2011; Powell & Murray 2008). Family violence appears to be perceived in gender-neutral terms as conflict between parents that can be resolved via mediation, without needing to impact on child custody decisions. Such a viewpoint is at odds with the domestic violence sector that recognises gendered power imbalances and prioritises women and children's rights to safety over family preservation. An approach that overlooks or trivialises family violence can also have fatal consequences for women and children. Take, for example, the case of 4-year-old Keira Jennifer Kagan in Toronto, Canada. On February 9, 2020, Kiera was killed by her biological father, Robin Brown, in an act of murder-suicide. Both parties were found dead at the bottom of Ontario Cliff after Brown had unsupervised custody of Keira that weekend. Brown had a history of perpetrating domestic violence against Keira's mother, but despite knowledge of domestic violence and abuse, the Judge, Justice Douglas Gray, awarded Brown liberal access to Keira, deeming the abuse as irrelevant to parenting.

Overall, it is clear that there is a lack of cohesive services and systems that impact children experiencing family violence. The shortcomings of each sector also potentially contribute to cultures that overlook or perpetuate child abuse. If the domestic violence sector is focused largely on adult women, the individual needs of children (e.g., post-crisis and therapeutic) may be going unmet. While child protection may focus on children, their broader culture around child removal may prevent women from seeking help from family violence, allowing abusive environments to continue. Moreover, children may be kept safe from familial violence by child protection, but there is also evidence that children placed in out-of-home care and residential care may experience child sexual abuse at higher rates than the general population (Euser et al. 2013). Finally, a family law system that minimises, disregards, and punishes reports of domestic violence and puts children into the unsupervised custody of abusive parents clearly creates a recipe for child abuse to occur. This is supported by research that has shown substantial rates of child abuse (including sexual abuse) in divorced families referred for child custody evaluations (Johnston et al. 2005). Each sector needs to turn the mirror on itself and consider how they can broaden their remit or better integrate with other services to ensure the ultimate safety of children. Team Leader, Shureeka Alves, articulated how dedicated children's sexual abuse agencies have struggled with the siloing of services but have seen improvements in recent years with the adoption of more integrated and client-centred approaches:

> I think there's been a culture where we see sexual abuse separate to family violence. There was a point in time when family violence was mentioned, you'd say right you need to go to a family violence service, [but] in the last 7 years, it has evolved. We know that a lot of young children that have been exposed to or witnessed family violence tend to display harmful sexual behaviours or are victims of sexual abuse.

This quote points to the problem of trying to compartmentalise children's traumatic experiences and distribute different aspects to separate services. It indicates how family violence and child sexual abuse are often intertwined and they need to be addressed in an integrated way. Shureeka also went on to describe how practitioner's identities can impact the scope of work they take on. She described how she used to view herself as working in the sexual abuse sector but given the overlapping nature of sexual abuse and family violence, she now considers herself a family violence practitioner because, "it goes hand in hand, you can't not see it combined together." Shureeka demonstrates how professional identities are malleable if individuals and sectors are open to adapting rather than having a rigid loyalty to original responsibilities. Adequate funding and training are also obvious requirements for sectors to be able to broaden their scope, build capacity, and integrate with other services effectively.

Conclusion: Family violence as the "perfect storm" for child sexual abuse

This chapter has shone a spotlight on child victims to illustrate the intersections of family violence and child abuse, with a focus on child sexual abuse. We saw how formal definitions of family violence are increasingly recognising the harm of exposing children to intimate partner violence. We also saw advocacy for a coercive control-based definition of domestic abuse to be applied to children. Coercive controlling environments appear to be breeding grounds for the perpetuation and concealment of child abuse. If children are isolated and disconnected from friends, family members, and other social networks, there is a lack of trusted people they can disclose abuse to and seek help from. This is particularly true for child sexual abuse, where there may not be any obvious signs for professionals or community members to detect:

> we can see a bruise and ask about the bruise and the child will tell us about the bruise because that's what they do but because we can't see child sexual abuse and we're not drawn to ask, it stays hidden.
>
> *Narelle Goodland, Principal Practitioner*

Overall, the empirical literature demonstrated a firm link between child abuse (including child sexual abuse) and intimate partner violence. Studies revealed high rates of co-occurrence and direct relationships between child sexual abuse, victimisation, and perpetration of intimate partner violence in adulthood. Research and our case studies also demonstrated how family violence is often multi-directional, with child victims of abuse also at a heightened risk of subjecting their siblings and parents to violence. It was evident that intimate partner violence can filter down to children, prompting negative social and psychological outcomes and problematic behaviours in childhood, that often persist into adulthood. Additionally, intimate partner violence creates conditions and dynamics that divert attention away from children, which ultimately contributes to the ongoing and hidden nature of child abuse. This was summed up by two of our interviewees who described family violence as the "perfect storm" and "perfect environment" for child sexual abuse to keep going (Narelle Goodland and Sarah Hill, respectively). Practitioners described how intimate partner violence can pre-occupy and distract adult victims from the abuse their children may be experiencing and overshadow children's abuse when first responders and service providers (e.g., police, social workers) are notified. Here Narelle elaborates further:

> The impetus has been understanding the child's experiences through the lens of mum or the woman or the affected family member, rather than direct engagement with children themselves. With that is a massive assumption that mum knows the harm that's happening to child, we know in child sexual abuse its highly likely she's not aware of what's actually happening.

The environments that enable child sexual abuse are no more apparent than in custody cases where abusive parents are granted unsupervised access or custody of children. This chapter examined the contradictions and limitations of services and systems that impact children, namely, the domestic violence, child protection, and family law sectors. It emphasised the need for more specialised children's services and better communication and integration of existing services, with a focus on cross-training to ensure professionals are aware of the issues that impact women and children in family violence contexts. It is essential that governments make substantial investments into services for children at all levels of prevention (primary, secondary, and tertiary). In sum, we need to see better education for children to understand the nature of family violence and child abuse, better opportunities to seek help, enhanced frontline responses to detect child abuse, improved support for families at risk of family violence, and more therapeutic and post-crisis services for children following abuse. We need to prioritise children if we want to see meaningful changes to rates of family violence and sexual offending.

References

Appel, A.E. and Holden, G.W., 1998. The co-occurrence of spouse and physical child abuse: A review and appraisal. *Journal of Family Psychology*, *12*(4), pp. 578–599.

Bidarra, Z.S., Lessard, G., and Dumont, A., 2016. Co-occurrence of intimate partner violence and child sexual abuse: Prevalence, risk factors and related issues. *Child Abuse & Neglect, 55*, pp. 10–21. doi:10.1016/j.chiabu.2016.03.007

Campbell, E., Richter, J., Howard, J., and Cockburn, H., 2020. *The PIPA project: Positive interventions for perpetrators of adolescent violence in the home (AVITH)*. Australia's National Research Organisation for Women's Safety (ANROWS), Sydney.

Campo, M., Kaspiew, R., Moore, S., and Tayton, S., 2014. *Children affected by domestic and family violence. A review of domestic and family violence prevention, early intervention and response services*. Australian Institute of Family Studies, Melbourne.

Cottrell, B. and Monk, P., 2004. Adolescent-to-parent abuse: A qualitative overview of common themes. *Journal of Family Issues, 25*(8), pp. 1072–1095. doi:10.1177/0192513X03261330

Daigneault, I., Hébert, M., and McDuff, P., 2009. Men's and women's childhood sexual abuse and victimization in adult partner relationships: A study of risk factors. *Child Abuse & Neglect, 33*(9), pp. 638–647. doi:10.1016/j.chiabu.2009.04.003

Daly, K. and Bouhours, B., 2010. Rape and attrition in the legal process: A comparative analysis of five countries. *Crime and Justice, 39*(1), pp. 565–650. doi:10.1086/653101

Donagh, B., 2020. From unnoticed to invisible: The impact of CoViD-19 on children and young people experiencing domestic violence and abuse. *Child Abuse Review, 29*(4), pp. 387–391. doi:10.1002/car.2649

Euser, S., Alink, L.R., Tharner, A., van IJzendoorn, M.H., and Bakermans-Kranenburg, M.J., 2013. The prevalence of child sexual abuse in out-of-home care: A comparison between abuse in residential and in foster care. *Child Maltreatment, 18*(4), pp. 221–231. doi:10.1177/1077559513489848

Fang, X. and Corso, P.S., 2007. Child maltreatment, youth violence, and intimate partner violence: Developmental relationships. *American Journal of Preventive Medicine, 33*(4), pp. 281–290. doi:10.1016/j.amepre.2007.06.003

Fitz-Gibbon, K., Elliott, K., and Maher, J., 2018. *Investigating adolescent family violence in Victoria: Understanding experiences and practitioner perspectives*. Monash University, Melbourne.

Fitz-Gibbon, K. and Meyer, S. 2021. *Two experts on how much the $1.1 billion for women's safety can achieve*. The Conversation, Melbourne.

Fry, D., McCoy, A., and Swales, D., 2012. The consequences of maltreatment on children's lives: A systematic review of data from the East Asia and Pacific Region. *Trauma, Violence, & Abuse, 13*(4), pp. 209–233. doi:10.1177/1524838012455873

Gallego, R., Novo, M., Fariña, F., and Arce, R., 2019. Child-to-parent violence and parent-to-child violence: A meta-analytic review. *European Journal of Psychology Applied to Legal Context, 11*(2), pp.51–59. doi:10.5093/ejpalc2019a4

Garcia-Linares, M.I., Pico-Alfonso, M.A., Sanchez-Lorente, S., Savall-Rodriguez, F., Celda-Navarro, N., Blasco-Ros, C., and Martinez, M., 2005. Assessing physical, sexual, and psychological violence perpetrated by intimate male partners toward women: A Spanish cross-sectional study. *Violence and Victims, 20*(1), pp. 99–123. doi:10.1089/jwh.2006.15.599

Goddard, C. and Bedi, G., 2010. Intimate partner violence and child abuse: A child-centred perspective. *Child Abuse Review: Journal of the British Association for the Study and Prevention of Child Abuse and Neglect, 19*(1), pp. 5–20. doi:10.1002/car.1084

Goddard, C.R. and Hiller, P. 1993. Child sexual abuse: Assault in a violent context. *The Australian Journal of Social Issues, 28*(1), pp. 20–33.

Hamby, S., Finkelhor, D., Turner, H., and Ormrod, R., 2010. The overlap of witnessing partner violence with child maltreatment and other victimizations in a nationally representative survey of youth. *Child Abuse & Neglect, 34*(10), pp. 734–741. doi:10.1016/j.chiabu.2010.03.001

Herrenkohl, T.I., Sousa, C., Tajima, E.A., Herrenkohl, R.C., and Moylan, C.A., 2008. Intersection of child abuse and children's exposure to domestic violence. *Trauma, Violence, & Abuse*, *9*(2), pp. 84–99. doi:10.1177/1524838008314797

Hester, M., 2011. The three planet model: Towards an understanding of contradictions in approaches to women and children's safety in contexts of domestic violence. *British Journal of Social Work*, *41*(5), pp.837–853. doi:10.1093/bjsw/bcr095

Hillis, S., Mercy, J., Amobi, A., and Kress, H., 2016. Global prevalence of past-year violence against children: A systematic review and minimum estimates. *Pediatrics*, *137*(3), pp. 1–22. doi:10.1542/peds.2015-4079

Hoffman, K.L., Kiecolt, K.J., and Edwards, J.N., 2005. Physical violence between siblings a theoretical and empirical analysis. *Journal of Family Issues*, *26*(8), pp. 1103–1130. doi:10.1177/0192513X05277809

Holt, A., 2012. *Adolescent-to-parent abuse: Current understandings in research, policy and practice*. Policy Press, Bristol.

Humphreys, C., 2008. Problems in the system of mandatory reporting of children living with domestic violence. *Journal of Family Studies*, *14*(2–3), pp. 228–239. doi:10.5172/jfs.327.14.2-3.228

Jennings, W.G., Richards, T.N., Tomsich, E., and Gover, A.R., 2015. Investigating the role of child sexual abuse in intimate partner violence victimization and perpetration in young adulthood from a propensity score matching approach. *Journal of Child Sexual Abuse*, *24*(6), pp. 659–681. doi:10.1080/10538712.2015.1057665

Johnston, J.R., Lee, S., Olesen, N.W., and Walters, M.G., 2005. Allegations and substantiations of abuse in custody-disputing families. *Family Court Review*, *43*(2), pp. 283–294. doi:10.1111/j.1744-1617.2005.00029.x

Katz, E., 2016. Beyond the physical incident model: How children living with domestic violence are harmed by and resist regimes of coercive control. *Child Abuse Review*, *25*(1), pp. 46–59. doi:10.1002/car.2422

Katz, E., Nikupeteri, A., and Laitinen, M., 2020. When coercive control continues to harm children: Post-separation fathering, stalking and domestic violence. *Child Abuse Review*, *29*(4), pp. 310–324. doi:10.1002/car.2611

Kennair, N. and Mellor, D., 2007. Parent abuse: A review. *Child Psychiatry and Human Development*, *38*(3), pp. 203–219. doi:10.1007/s10578-007-0061-x

Langton, M., Smith, K., Eastman, T., O'Neill, L., Cheesman, E., and Rose, M. 2020. *Improving family violence legal and support services for Aboriginal and Torres Strait Islander women*. ANROWS, Sydney.

Macy, R.J., Giattina, M.C., Montijo, N.J., and Ermentrout, D.M., 2010. Domestic violence and sexual assault agency directors' perspectives on services that help survivors. *Violence against Women*, *16*(10), pp. 1138–1161. doi:10.1177/1077801210383085

Meyer, S. 2020. *Why we need to focus more on the needs of children in domestic and family violence responses*. Monash University, Melbourne.

National Crime Agency. 2020. *Law enforcement in coronavirus online safety push as National Crime Agency reveals 300,000 in UK pose sexual threat to children*. London.

Powell, A. and Murray, S., 2008. Children and domestic violence: Constructing a policy problem in Australia and New Zealand. *Social & Legal Studies*, *17*(4), pp. 453–473. doi:10.1177/0964663908097080

RAINN, 2021. *Children and teens: Statistics*. Rape, Abuse & Incest National Network, Washington.

Renner, L.M. and Slack, K.S., 2006. Intimate partner violence and child maltreatment: Understanding intra-and intergenerational connections. *Child Abuse & Neglect*, *30*(6), pp. 599–617. doi:10.1016/j.chiabu.2005.12.005

Renner, L.M. and Whitney, S.D., 2012. Risk factors for unidirectional and bidirectional intimate partner violence among young adults. *Child Abuse & Neglect*, *36*(1), pp. 40–52. doi:10.1016/j.chiabu.2011.07.007

Saunders, D.G., Faller, K.C., and Tolman, R.M., 2012. *Child custody evaluators' beliefs about domestic abuse allegations: Their relationship to evaluator demographics, background, domestic violence knowledge and custody-visitation recommendations: Final technical report submitted to the National Institute of Justice, US Department of Justice*. National Criminal Justice Reference Service, Washington.

Stewart, M., Burns, A., and Leonard, R., 2007. Dark side of the mothering role: Abuse of mothers by adolescent and adult children. *Sex Roles*, *56*(3), pp. 183–191. doi:10.1007/s11199-006-9148-2

Widom, C.S., Czaja, S., and Dutton, M.A., 2014. Child abuse and neglect and intimate partner violence victimization and perpetration: A prospective investigation. *Child Abuse & Neglect*, *38*(4), pp. 650–663. doi:10.1016/j.chiabu.2013.11.004

6

PUNISHMENT AND TREATMENT OF OFFENDERS

Do we have equal responses?

As we have seen in previous chapters, there are many similarities between family violence and sexual offending, with sexual violence often being part and parcel of family violence. Yet distinct conceptualisations endure, and these are particularly evident at the tail end of the criminal justice system where punishments and treatments for offenders are dealt. In the last chapter, i.e., Conclusion, we turn our eye to the court processes, attrition, and conviction rates involved in family violence and sexual offence cases. We provide critical and comparative commentary on the various criminal justice and treatment options available to those charged with family violence and/or sexual offences, ultimately arguing that those considered "family violence" perpetrators are treated more leniently by the criminal justice system compared to those considered "sex offenders." We also highlight the many paradoxes in how we respond, or profess to respond, to sexual crime at the tertiary prevention stage. Here, our intention is not to promote a carceral response; there are clearly negative and counterproductive consequences for harsher criminal justice penalties, especially for marginalised groups. Rather, our aim is to draw attention to the imbalances between our formal justice responses to family violence and sexual crime and consider *why* and what this might mean for future policies and procedures.

Attrition and conviction rates

It is well established that sexual offences have high attrition rates from the criminal justice process and alarmingly low conviction rates across the world (Daly & Bouhours 2010). Indeed, recent available data from Victoria, Australia shows that less than 8% of reported rapes involving adult victims resulted in a conviction (Bright et al. 2021) and in the last decade across Australia, police resolved approximately 25% of sexual assault cases (n = 34,000) without making an arrest or taking

DOI: 10.4324/9781003051657-7

any legal action (Ting, Scott, & Palmer 2020). These figures are dire, especially given the initial reporting rate to police is so low: approximately 3 million Australians over the age of 18 have experienced sexual violence but only 13% of victim-survivors have reported to police (ABS 2021). The sexual offences resulting in a conviction are only the very tip of the iceberg.

Likewise, rape prosecutions and convictions have fallen to an all-time low in England and Wales leading many organisations and commentators to point out that rape has essentially been decriminalised in the United Kingdom (The Centre for Women's Justice et al. 2020). Similar trends are evident in the United States, where 97.5% of people who perpetrate sexual assault do not serve time in prison (RAINN 2020). A huge backlog of untested rape kits is currently one of the largest hurdles preventing the timely prosecution of sexual offences in America. It is estimated that there are currently over 100,000 untested rape kits in the United States, with studies showing that serial offenders could have been identified if the rape kit evidence had been sent to a crime lab for testing (Curington 2021). Such trends clearly demonstrate the criminal justice systems' failure in responding to victim-survivors of sexual offences, and beg the question as seen in the title of Michele Bowdler's memoir and manifesto, "Is Rape a Crime?" (Bowdler 2020).

Securing a criminal justice outcome is even more difficult for sexual offences when they are perpetrated by someone known to the victim versus a stranger. Studies have recurringly indicated that sexual assaults by strangers are more likely to progress through the criminal justice system and are treated more seriously by criminal justice stakeholders than those involving acquaintances and intimate partners (Bright et al. 2021; Spohn & Tellis 2012). As we saw in Chapter 3, rape myths and stereotypes about "real rapes" involving strangers persist in the community, including among professionals and decision-makers in the criminal justice system. They manifest during case processing whereby police and prosecutors more heavily scrutinise the credibility of the victim's character and behaviour in sexual offence cases involving acquaintances, relatives, and intimate partners compared to strangers (Spohn & Holleran 2001). Ultimately, this leads to more obstacles for victims and less accountability for perpetrators of intimate partner sexual violence, or sexual violence occurring in a family context.

While it is now well-known that sexual offences are marked by high attrition and low conviction rates, the treatment of family violence cases by the criminal justice system is less clear. There are few studies that have tracked the case processing of family violence cases on a large scale. Most available studies appear to adopt a "micro-level" approach where they track a smaller sample of offences. The main challenge in tracking family violence cases is that most offences are charged as discrete incidents and classified according to the offence type rather than the relationship between the victim and perpetrator. For example, offences may be recorded as homicide, assault, rape, threats, abduction, etc. Moreover, many family violence offences reported to police do not necessarily require a conviction and/or custodial sentence, making it more difficult to clearly track and make conclusions about attrition and conviction rates (Chopin & Aebi 2020). This raises implications for how we record family violence offences in formal databases, as a clear tracking system is necessary for evaluation purposes.

Countries that have attempted to track family violence convictions have shown mixed trends. For example, Poland, Switzerland, and the United Kingdom have all shown high attrition rates (80% and higher) and low conviction rates (20% and lower) for domestic violence and abuse offences (Chopin & Aebi 2020; Grzyb 2020). A study of 135 reports, mostly from the United States, found that on average one-third of reported intimate partner violence offences resulted in the filing of charges, and more than half of all prosecutions resulted in a criminal conviction (Garner & Maxwell 2009). Since Scotland have implemented their new coercive control laws, they have seen high conviction rates (84%) with convictions expected to rise in future years (Scottish Government 2021). Despite the variability among jurisdictions, data suggest that family violence offences are less likely to drop out of the criminal justice process and are more likely to result in convictions or criminal justice outcomes than sexual offences alone. This is perhaps not surprising given there may be more evidence in intimate partner violence cases to corroborate victim statements (e.g., witnesses, body-worn camera footage from first responders, injuries, phone records) compared to sexual violence cases where the victim's statement is often the only core piece of evidence, and it can be difficult to establish medically whether sexual activity was consensual or not.

The above data may paint a picture that we respond more severely to family violence cases than sexual offence cases alone. Yet, what we will see in the next section is that there are far more civil remedies and community-based treatment options for offenders charged with family violence offences compared to sexual offences. In parallel, we have mostly custodial sentences and treatments for perpetrators of sexual crimes, but the chances of perpetrators ever entering custody are slim. This means that we are taking sexual crimes seriously in theory and in policy, but the low conviction rates suggest this is not translating into practise. In other words, the vast majority of sex offenders are walking free in our community, never having received any punishment or treatment.

Criminal justice options and treatment programmes

A critical appraisal of the criminal justice responses to family violence versus sexual offences reveals several themes. Firstly, the criminal justice options for perpetrators of family violence are much more diverse than for people considered "sex offenders." In Victoria, Australia for example, someone charged with family violence may be issued with a safety notice (a temporary intervention order issued by police until a decision can be made by the court), an interim or a final intervention order granted by a court that requires the perpetrator to stop the violent behaviour and may cease them from contacting or visiting the protected person. The court may also suspend or cancel the perpetrator's firearm licence. The intervention orders are considered civil matters but can turn into criminal matters if the conditions are breached.

Similar processes are seen in other parts of the world (e.g., protective orders in the United States).

Over the last decade in Victoria, we have also seen the rollout of specialist Family Violence courts with dedicated magistrates, support workers, and outreach services for victims and perpetrators, and additional safety measures. After an intervention order has been granted, a magistrate can also order that a perpetrator attends counselling, a Respectful Relationships, or Men's Behaviour Change Program. Such programmes are based on the Duluth model from the United States, a coordinated community response which emphasises victim safety and perpetrator accountability (Shepard & Pence 1999). Generally, the programmes are group-based and total about 40 hours of therapeutic intervention spaced over 14 to 24 weeks. Facilitators provide psychoeducation with the aim of changing attitudes and behaviours, with some programmes also offering victim safety planning and support. Participation in a Men's Behavioural Change Program can be mandated or based on a referral from the perpetrator or an agency. Research suggests, however, that full completion of such programmes is low (Victorian Government 2018).

Other penalties for family violence vary according to the severity of the offence or breach of order. Perpetrators may receive a warning, fine, an adjourned undertaking (good behaviour bond where offender may be released without a recorded conviction if they promise to be of good behaviour for a designated period), a community corrections order, suspended sentence or imprisonment. Generally, we have seen the trend that breaches of intervention orders are treated leniently with lower-end orders, if anything at all (Hawkins & Broughton 2016). In many cases, this has led to devasting consequences. For example, in Australia, Hannah Clark and her three children Aaliya, Lainah, and Trey were killed when Hannah's ex-husband set the family on fire. The perpetrator had breached an intervention order several times but had not received a swift or firm response from the criminal justice system to keep the family safe.

In contrast to the array of options for perpetrators of family violence, the criminal justice response options for those charged with sexual offences are narrower and appear harsher. If charged with a sex offence, the main course of action is an adversarial penalty resulting in a custodial sentence, and to a lesser degree, community corrections orders, and suspended sentences. In some jurisdictions (e.g., Alabama, the United States), those found guilty of certain sex offences may face mandated chemical castration or voluntary surgical castration. Following a sentence, offenders may be subject to electronic monitoring and may be placed on a sex offender registry which often limits where they can live or work, as well as other activities such as social media use.

There tends to be disparity in the length of prison sentences imposed for sex offences versus family violence offences. Scotland provides us with a good opportunity for comparison as they have legislation that criminalises patterns of domestic abuse rather than just discrete incidents. For example, the Domestic Abuse Act in Scotland criminalises coercive controlling behaviours which encompasses sexual abuse. This carries a maximum 14-year sentence. In contrast, the offences of rape and sexual assault carry a maximum penalty of life imprisonment. This is not to say that a domestic abuser cannot also be charged with rape, but the legislation presents an interesting discrepancy that is perhaps telling of how we perceive and tolerate sexual violence in different contexts. That is, we are more accepting and less likely to formally condemn sexual violence when it occurs within domestic settings. Since the Domestic Abuse legislation was enacted in 2019, community sentences have been the most common penalty (61%). Of those with custodial sentences (19%), the average sentence length was about one year. Conversely, those found guilty of rape or attempted rape were overwhelmingly sentenced to custody (98%) with an average sentence length of 6 years and 8 months (Scottish Government 2021).

Most treatment programmes for those considered "sex offenders" are mandated as part of a custodial sentence. Namely, the programme is delivered in a prison setting, with some programmes delivered in an outreach or community format, but mostly for those who are reintegrating back into the community (e.g., Circles of Support). Treatment programmes within prisons are commonly run by multidisciplinary professionals such as social workers, psychologists, and corrective services officers in a group setting. Based on the Risk Needs Responsivity model, programmes are mostly targeted at moderate- to high-risk offenders and have a particular focus on cognitive behavioural therapy (Grealy et al. 2013).

Unlike coordinated community responses to family violence, treatment programmes for sex offenders rarely involve the victim. Restorative justice practises have only just been established for serious violent and sexual crime, here in Victoria, despite being available in some countries for decades. This is also notwithstanding clear evidence that all parties involved in restorative processes, whether offender or victim, report high satisfaction rates, and find the process to be fair. Restorative justice reduces victims fear, as well as anger towards offenders (Centre for Innovative Justice 2014). The rollout of restorative justice in Victoria, late as it is, offers insight into how differently we see the needs of victims, and our requirements for justice responses. For example, early services, much like early therapeutic intervention for those who commit sexual offences, were directed at young people. When adult services were developed, they were not initially seen as suitable for interpersonal crimes, with the view predominating that the community expected more rigorous punishment. When this argument also gave way, family violence was seen as the first port of call, with restorative justice felt to be more appropriate for this type of offending behaviour over sexual offences.

The menu of criminal justice response and treatment options for family violence and sexual offences is indicative of how we view the two types of offending. In general, the medical-psychological model that guides sex offender treatment signals how we still view sexual offending as an individual pathological problem, with less emphasis on social and situational antecedents. We assume there must be something inherent within the perpetrator that explains their offending and distinguishes them from others within society. This is despite the fact that most sexual offenders are not mentally ill, and most child sex offenders do not meet the *APA Diagnostic and Statistical Manual of Mental Disorders'* diagnosis of paedophilia

(Gelb 2007; Richards 2011). Alternatively, family violence programmes seem to have a much greater weight put on psycho-social and broader contextual factors related to offending.

Similarly, the lack of community-based programmes for perpetrators of sexual crimes indicates our continued distrust in sex offender's ability to cease offending. Family violence perpetrators are given many chances, but sex offenders are not afforded the same opportunities for redemption. This is paradoxical because the rates of sexual recidivism are quite low: 5–15% after 5 years and 10–25% after 10+ years (cumulatively, keeping in mind, however, that these figures are based on recorded data which we know are an under-representation: Scurich & John 2019). Nevertheless, research suggests that recidivism for sexual offending tends to be lower than for other violent crimes (e.g., Jones et al. 2006; Mercado et al. 2013). In other words, the majority of sex offenders do not re-enter the criminal justice system for sexual recidivism, whereas the same cannot be said for family violence perpetrators who frequently reoffend (Hulme, Morgan, & Boxall 2019). For example, one Victorian study found that one in two family violence perpetrators (51%) were involved in at least one other recorded incident within four years (Millsteed 2016).

Further, our willingness to have family violence offenders serve penalties or treatments in the community, but not "sex offenders," fails to acknowledge that many family violence offenders are sex offenders. As we have seen throughout this book, sexual violence and abuse is often a key part of a domestic abuser's toolbox. For instance, one U.S. study found that almost 40% of women who had obtained a protective order against a male partner had experienced intimate partner sexual violence (Cole, Logan, & Shannon 2005). Why, then, are we so reluctant to think of domestic abusers as sex offenders? Why do we persist with such different conceptualisations when we know both are cut from the same cloth? Let us reflect on this further with the following two cases:

Case study 1

A university student, living in university accommodation, reports threatening texts messages and stalking behaviour from an ex-partner. They also detail, when reporting to university authorities, that there were physical abuses during the relationship. They do not want to pursue a report to police but want to let the ex-partner know about the impact of his behaviour and prompt him to seek therapeutic assistance for their behaviour.

Case study 2

A university student, living in university accommodation, reports threatening texts messages and stalking behaviour from an ex-partner. They also detail, when reporting to university authorities, that they were subjected to non-consensual sexual acts during the relationship. They do not want to pursue a

> report to police but want to let the ex-partner know about the impact of his behaviour and prompt him to seek therapeutic assistance for their behaviour.

Although all victims' experience of abuse is unique, and the impacts of sexual abuse and the relationship can have significant variation, the trauma impact of these behaviours have many more similarities than differences. Both sets of crimes are unlikely to be reported, or to reach the adversarial courts. We also know that intimate partner violence and sexual offending share many of the same gendered drivers. According to the Australian "Change the Story Framework," violence against women stems from gender inequality, often expressed in key ways: (i) condoning of violence against women, (ii) men's control of decision-making and limits to women's independence in public and private life, (iii) rigid gender roles and stereotypes constructions of masculinity and femininity, and (iv) male peer relations that emphasise aggression and disrespect towards women (Our Watch, ANROWS, & VicHealth 2015). Reinforcing factors also include the condoning of violence in general; experience of, and exposure to violence; weakening of prosocial behaviour, especially harmful use of alcohol; socio-economic inequality and discrimination; as well as backlash factors (e.g., when male dominance, power, or status is challenged).

Decades of psychological and criminological research has also shown that the aetiology of violent and sexual offending is remarkably similar. For example, "the central eight" are well-known criminogenic factors that are predictive of serious offending. These comprise (1) a history of antisocial behaviour, (2) an antisocial personality, (3) antisocial attitudes, (4) antisocial peers, (5) substance abuse, (6) poor family and/or marital relationships, (7) lack of strong employment and education, and (8) a lack of involvement in prosocial leisure activities (Andrews & Bonta 2010). Therefore, a melting pot of individual, social, and environmental factors contribute to a person's likelihood of engaging in serious offending. Their offending tendencies are routed in similar origins, but as described by Australian forensic psychologist, Simone Shaw, what differs is their choice of "weapon" at the end. They may choose to exert violence, power, and control through physical violence, sexual violence, or a combination of both.

Despite sharing many similarities, it is curious that we continue to view and treat family violence and sexual offending so differently. A discord in our response can also be seen in family violence training and programmes. There is seldom explicit mention of sexual violence in treatment programmes for domestic abusers. It is common for behaviour change programmes to target family violence or sexual offending but, "few are structured in a way to acknowledge the high rate of co-occurrence in the form of intimate partner sexual violence" (Cox 2015). Sharon Simon, an industry fellow in family violence, points out that in family violence training, sexual assault is mentioned as a risk factor but is rarely unpacked further than that. This was also echoed by another of our interviewees, a family violence crisis worker, who confirmed she had not received any training in sexual violence. Here she elaborates further:

> If someone has come to us and they've experienced sexual violence and they want specialist support with sexual violence, we will refer them to [de-identified service], because myself, my organisation and I'm assuming other organisations like me that specialise just in family violence, we're not given that training to address sexual violence. It's like there's someone out there for you, so its not integrated, which I think is a massive gap—it makes it very tricky for victim-survivors to seek support as well.

There are, of course, unique aspects of family violence and sexual offending that require deeper levels of specialisation. But as we have seen throughout this book, there are many similarities and overlaps that require attention. In the subsequent and final chapter, we will also see there is a significant need for greater cross-pollination between the two sectors. This is particularly apparent for the criminal justice system, which currently adopts a very siloed and distinct approach to responding to family violence and sexual violence.

Closing remarks and future directions

So, do we have equal responses in how we treat and respond to perpetrators of family and/or sexual violence? Let it be clear, both crimes have a history and indeed continuing legacy of low reporting, prosecution, and conviction. Both are often treated as private issues and there are countless examples where police and courts have not taken such crimes seriously, resulting in devastating consequences, often for women and children. The criminal justice (or injustice) system clearly and routinely fails victim-survivors of both family violence and sexual offending.

As a potential reflection and extension of society's broader views, however, the criminal justice system appears to be more accepting and lenient with family violence compared to sexual offending. Generally, we give family violence perpetrators more chances, and have an array of civil remedies and treatments which we trust offenders to undertake within the community. This contrasts with the more limited and stringent custodial measures for sex offences (at least in the cases of sexual offending by strangers or cases that fit the "real rape" mould). We recognise sexual violence as part of the legal definition of family violence and/or coercive control, yet we are willing to overlook this aspect and rarely pursue it in the criminal justice context. This is evident in sentence lengths in legislation, as well as notable attrition rates for cases of intimate partner sexual violence.

We also see that the criminal justice response to sexual crime is largely contradictory. On the one hand we are happy to give many alleged sexual offenders the benefit of the doubt, as seen in the particularly high drop-off rate of cases at the police investigative stage (Daly & Bouhours 2010). If a case happens to squeeze its way to trial, the benchmark for a conviction is almost unattainable. As highlighted by Bri Lee (2018) in her memoir, Eggshell Skull:

> As usual, there was barely any other "evidence." It was painful sometimes to see the looks on jurors' faces when they realised they wouldn't get any CCTV footage or CSI-style DNA tests. It is the absolute catch-22: people feel they need certain types of evidence to feel comfortable convicting a defendant of a crime, but crimes against women and children are usually committed inside homes by people they know... It's so easy for them [jurors] to say that "her word alone" wasn't enough to overcome their reasonable doubts.

On the other hand, when a case results in a conviction, the sanctions generally signal our disdain and repulsion of such crime. There are of course exceptions, mostly for privileged white males (e.g., Brock Turner), but in general, once labelled a "sex offender," our collective and criminal justice response emphasises punishment and retribution over deterrence and rehabilitation. Stereotypes about sexual offenders clearly prevail and influence criminal justice responses and treatment programmes. It is here we must be careful. While longer and stricter sentences point to our condemnation of sexual crime, decades of research has shown that prison does little to deter crime, and can actually increase ones propensity for further offending (see Petrich et al. 2021 for a robust criminological meta-analytic reviews in history). It is also well documented that the criminal justice system can be a significant source of pain and trauma for victim-survivors.

In moving forward, it is clear we must strive for the right balance of offender accountability and justice for victims, with an emphasis on evidence-based policies and treatment programmes that serve to rehabilitate and reduce reoffending. As we saw in Chapter 2, politics are closely intertwined with criminal justice responses to family violence and sexual offending, but we must ensure we are doing what is in the best long-term interests of the community, rather than exploiting community outrage to gain popularity and win votes. Restorative, therapeutic, and other alternative justice pathways offer promising future directions for both family violence and sexual offending (e.g., see Centre for Innovative Justice 2014 and Henry, Powell, & Flynn 2015). While relatively recent innovations for both types of offending, restorative approaches to sexual offending continue to lag behind family violence.

Primary prevention is also a vital mission that requires ongoing investment. As part of these prevention efforts, it is important we continue to break down stubborn stereotypes about "real" sex offenders if we are to truly prevent sexual violence, within and outside of relationship settings. Increasing community understandings of family violence and sexual offending is likely to have implications for all areas of the criminal justice system. For example, in Australia, three-quarters of female sexual assault victim-survivors do not immediately realise they have been assaulted (ABS 2021). Greater understandings of consent and sexual violence may influence initial reporting rates either to police or anonymous reporting avenues. Likewise, more education and training for criminal justice professionals and legal adjudicators may influence the downstream orientation and final verdicts of cases (e.g., see

Tidmarsh, Hamilton, & Sharman 2020 for our study on intensive training that can change police attitudes and decision-making in sexual offence cases).

Overall, this chapter has demonstrated that we do not have equal justice responses to family violence and sexual offending. Differing trends reflect discrepancies in how we view such crimes throughout, and particularly at the backend of the adversarial and correctional system. This clearly has implications for different types of crimes, especially for cases of sexual violence that occur within familial and intimate partner relationships, which are often rendered invisible in the criminal justice context. Because family violence and sexual offending are so interlaced, we emphasise the consideration of more cohesive criminal and restorative justice responses. The subsequent and concluding chapter offers further insight into such advancements.

References

ABS, 2021. *Recorded crime – Victims*. Australian Bureau of Statistics, Canberra.

Andrews, D.A. and Bonta, J., 2010. *The psychology of criminal conduct*. Routledge, New York.

Bowdler, M., 2020. *Is rape a crime?: A memoir, an investigation, and a manifesto*. Flatiron Books, New York.

Bright, S., Roach, C., Barnaba, L., Walker, S., and Millsteed, M., 2021. *Attrition of sexual offence incidents through the Victorian criminal justice system*. Crime Statistics Agency, Melbourne.

Centre for Innovative Justice, 2014. Innovative justice responses to sexual offending–pathways to better outcomes for victims, offenders and the community. RMIT University, Melbourne.

Chopin, J. and Aebi, M.F., 2020. The level of attrition in domestic violence: A valid indicator of the efficiency of a criminal justice system? *European Journal of Criminology, 17*(3), pp. 269–287. doi:10.1177/1477370818792477

Cole, J., Logan, T.K., and Shannon, L., 2005. Intimate sexual victimization among women with protective orders: Types and associations of physical and mental health problems. *Violence and Victims, 20*(6), pp. 695–715. doi:10.1891/0886-6708.20.6.695

Cox, P., 2015. *Sexual assault and domestic violence in the context of co-occurrence and re-victimisation state of knowledge*. ANROWS, Sydney.

Curington, M., 2021. *The injustice of America's rape kit backlog*. The Arkansas Journal of Social Change and Public Service, Little Rock.

Daly, K. and Bouhours, B., 2010. Rape and attrition in the legal process: A comparative analysis of five countries. *Crime and Justice, 39*(1), pp. 565–650. doi:10.1086/653101

Garner, J.H. and Maxwell, C.D., 2009. Prosecution and conviction rates for intimate partner violence. *Criminal Justice Review, 34*(1), pp. 44–79. doi:10.1177/0734016808324231

Gelb, K., 2007. *Recidivism of sex offenders research paper*. Sentencing Advisory Council, Melbourne.

Grealy, C., Wallace, A., Wilczynski, A., Lai, S., Bodiam, T., Dowler, B., and Jones, L., 2013. *Literature review on domestic violence perpetrators*. Urbis Pty Ltd, Melbourne.

Grzyb, M., 2020. 'We condemn abusing violence against women'. The criminalisation of domestic violence in Poland. *Archives of Criminology, 1*(XLII), pp. 163–183. doi:10.7420/AK2020I

Hawkins, K. and Broughton, F., 2016. *Sentencing in family violence cases*. Current Issues in Sentencing–National Judicial College of Australia Conference, Victoria.

Hulme, S., Morgan, A., and Boxall, H., 2019. Domestic violence offenders, prior offending and reoffending in Australia. *Trends and Issues in Crime and Criminal Justice, 580*, pp. 1–22.

Jones, C., Hua, J., Donnelly, N., McHutchison, J., and Heggie, K., 2006. Risk of re-offending among parolees. *Crime and Justice Bulletin*, (91), pp. 1–12.

Henry, N., Powell, A., and Flynn, A. eds., 2015. *Rape justice: Beyond the criminal law*. Palgrave Macmillan, London.

Lee, B., 2018. *Eggshell skull*. Allen & Unwin, Melbourne.

Mercado, C.C., Jeglic, E., Markus, K., Hanson, K.R., and Levenson. J., 2013. *Sex offender management, treatment, and civil commitment: An evidence based analysis aimed at reducing sexual violence*. Research Report Submitted to the National Institute of Justice.

Millsteed, M., 2016. *How many repeat family violence perpetrators were there in Victoria over the past 10 years?* Fact no. 2, Crime Statistics Agency, Melbourne.

Our Watch, ANROWS, and VicHealth, 2015. *Change the story: A shared framework for the primary prevention of violence against women and their children in Australia*. Our Watch, Melbourne.

Petrich, D.M., Pratt, T.C., Jonson, C.L., and Cullen, F.T., 2021. Custodial sanctions and reoffending: A meta-analytic review. *Crime and Justice, 50*(1), pp. 1-64. doi:10.1086/715100

RAINN, 2020. *The criminal justice system: Statistics*. Rape, Abuse & Incest National Network, Washington.

Richards, K., 2011. Misperceptions about child sex offenders. *Trends and Issues in Crime and Criminal Justice, 429*, pp. 1–8.

Scottish Government, 2021. *Criminal proceedings in Scotland, 2019–2020*. Scotland. ISBN:9781800049628

Scurich, N. and John, R.S., 2019. The dark figure of sexual recidivism. *Behavioral Sciences & the Law, 37*(2), pp. 158–175. doi:10.1002/bsl.2400

Shepard, M.F. and Pence, E.L. eds., 1999. *Coordinating community responses to domestic violence: Lessons from Duluth and beyond*. Sage, New York.

Spohn, C. and Holleran, D., 2001. Prosecuting sexual assault: A comparison of charging decisions in sexual assault cases involving strangers, acquaintances, and intimate partners. *Justice Quarterly, 18*(3), pp. 651–688. Doi:10.1080/07418820100095051

Spohn, C. and Tellis, K., 2012. The criminal justice system's response to sexual violence. *Violence against Women, 18*(2), pp. 169–192. Doi:10.1177/1077801212440020

The Centre for Women's Justice, End Violence against Women, Imkaan, and Rape Crisis England and Wales, 2020. *The decriminalisation of rape: Why the justice system is failing rape survivors and what needs to change*. England and Wales.

Tidmarsh, P., Hamilton, G., and Sharman, S.J., 2020. Changing police officers' attitudes in sexual offense cases: A 12-month follow-up study. *Criminal Justice and Behavior, 47*(9), pp. 1176–1189. Doi:10.1177/0093854820921201

Ting, I., Scott, N., and Palmer, A., 2020. *Rough justice: How police are failing survivors of sexual assault*. ABC News, Sydney.

Victorian Government, 2018. *Expert advisory committee on perpetrator interventions: Final report* (1925789144). Victoria State Government, Melbourne.

CONCLUSION

Family violence and sexual offending are critical global problems. As we have seen throughout this book, they are highly interrelated issues, but the nexus between family violence and sexual offending is often not well conceptualised or operationalised in policy and practise, particularly in social service and criminal justice responses. At times throughout history, family violence and sexual offending have leapfrogged each other in academic and government attention, but we appear to be making progress in terms of a more coordinated approach. In this conclusion, we draw together the key messages and learnings from each chapter. We summarise implications of current frameworks for preventing and responding to family and sexual violence, with a focus on co-located and cross-pollination models. We also provide recommendations for future research and practise, ending with a critical but optimistic view on how we can maintain the two lenses and ultimately strengthen our approaches to these intersecting harms.

In Chapter 1 we explored the different languages adopted in family violence and sexual offending sectors, signalling similar perpetrator behaviours and room for the coercive control field to recognise the crossover with grooming. Particular attention was paid to intimate partner sexual violence, highlighting the need for a distinct and uniform definition that recognises the unique harm its poses for victim-survivors. At the core of intimate partner sexual violence lies a context where open and free consent cannot be given. Summed up soundly by victim-survivor and advocate, Geraldine Bilston, "I now know that there cannot be consent where there is this level of coercion. There is serious harm that occurs when psychological abuse intersects with a person's sexual autonomy" (2021).

Chapter 2 reflected on the political landscapes and bureaucratic processes that shape policies and funding structures to address family and sexual violence. We saw that at times, top-down decisions are made arbitrarily, and at other times made consciously, with a wilful ignorance towards sexual violence. This is often tied to public

DOI: 10.4324/9781003051657-8

perceptions and misconceptions regarding family violence and sexual offending uncovered in Chapter 3. But such decisions have significant implications for the structure and functioning of services, and, in turn, victim-survivors' lives. Here, we call for increased funding so that governments are not receiving a two-for-one discount when it comes to budgets for family and sexual violence—issues that frequently and overwhelmingly impact women and children.

In Chapter 4, we examined the intersections of family violence and sexual offending in the context of policing. It was evident that policing organisations often respond to family and sexual violence in a disjointed way, despite the significant overlap in these crimes. Victims' reports are put into a figurative sorting hat and directed to different branches of police with different investigative priorities. This can create conditions where certain crimes might be overlooked. For example, officers frequently do not ask about or pursue sexual violence charges as part of an investigation into family violence. A disjointed approach also inhibits the ability to detect and respond to children's abuse. In Chapter 5, we saw that intimate partner violence often creates the "perfect storm" for child sexual abuse to occur. It creates conditions and dynamics that divert attention away from children, which ultimately contributes to the ongoing and hidden nature of such abuse. In moving forward, prevention efforts need to centre children's experiences to see meaningful changes in rates of family violence and sexual offending.

Finally, in Chapter 6, we cast a critical light on the inconsistencies in our criminal justice responses to family and sexual violence. We contend that conceptualisations of perpetrators as "sex offenders" versus "family violence offenders" influence their penalties and treatment options, with substantiated family violence generally treated more leniently than substantiated sexual offending. Again, this stems from the myriad of societal myths and misconceptions about perpetrators and their behaviours. So where to from here? What type of service model is going to work effectively for victim-survivors of family and/or sexual violence?

Co-located models

Given the high overlap of family violence and sexual offending, a combined model makes sense. A single service provider promotes accessibility for victims rather than referring them out and requiring them to navigate a complex array of different services. Victim-survivors do not need further stress and complication at an already complicated time of their life. As we highlighted in Chapter 2, victims do not tend to compartmentalise their abuse and put it into discrete columns to be addressed neatly by different services. They consistently report wanting holistic and coordinated help (Koss, White, & Lopez 2017).

There is also significant overlap in the nature of services provided by family and sexual violence organisations. Team leader at Kids First Australia, Shureeka Alves, reflected in one of our interviews, "Actually you know what, when you come to think of it, there's nothing really different." She elaborated that both sectors engage in risk assessment, safety planning, and address the impacts of family violence. They also both operate under frameworks that are trauma-informed, family focused, and client-centred, often under the same theoretical umbrella of feminism. Similarities between family and sexual violence services were also realised in research in the United States, highlighting both sectors adopt similar goals, service strategies, and service components (e.g., crisis services, counselling, telephone lines, support groups: Macy et al. 2009). At the heart of both services is an aim to improve victim's safety and well-being.

Co-located models for family and sexual violence are largely underscored by positive feedback from victim-survivors and stakeholders. For example, victims tend to report high satisfaction and positive outcomes following help-seeking at a co-located centre (e.g., greater hope, empowerment, and improved well-being). Likewise, stakeholders generally report positive impressions and experiences of providing services in co-located centres (Rizo et al. 2021). This was evident in our interview with Sarah Hill, a counsellor and advocate at a co-located centre, who described the benefits of a joined-up approach:

> If I have recognised a recent sexual assault in a client who has walked in the front door, I can just walk into the other room and there's a resource right there, a worker who can respond with that skillset in real time and then once that part has been addressed, we can pick up with the safety planning and the resources in keeping the victim-survivor safe, all the way through the process in one organisation and that person doesn't have to then tell their story a million times.

While a co-located centre is a promising model that addresses the shortcomings of traditional siloed approaches, we must also be mindful of the potential limitations it presents. A major concern expressed in the literature and by our stakeholder interviewees is the potential for sexual violence services to be diluted and overshadowed by the immediate nature of family violence work. Sexual assault agency directors fear they will end up seeing fewer victims and have even less time to promote rape crisis services in the community if their services are merged with the family violence sector (Macy et al. 2010). There is a worry that if sexual violence services accept funding from overarching family violence organisations, they will be flooded with family violence work when they already have a high volume of clients who experience sexual violence outside of the domestic and family violence context (e.g., historical survivors of child sexual abuse).

This is where we see the key differences in family violence and sexual violence work emerge. Family violence social service responses tend to involve more crisis work, risk assessment, and safety planning (e.g., organising shelter and housing). If a sexual assault has been recent (e.g., within last 48 hours), sexual violence responses can also involve crisis work and safety planning, but the bulk of sexual violence work comprises long-term therapeutic work to help with healing. While all these services are vital, the crisis family violence work ends up taking precedence, and therapeutic work is often put on the backburner to be dealt with at a later time.

Counsellor and Advocate, Rebecca, passionately articulates the problem with this approach:

> Following family violence, a lot of survivors are at peak crisis. This person doesn't have housing, they're living in a refuge… but there's this weird assumption that to do therapeutic work in the sexual assault space, "all your ducks need to be in a row." I often feel that people are saying "well they've got to be stable" – and yes to some degree there needs to be, Maslow's Hierarchy, if you haven't got somewhere to sleep and you're not eating then it is hard to engage in a counselling service but I certainly think that there are things we can provide in that space.
>
> Focusing only on family violence has downsides because we're still having conversations about how awful it is to be stalked or killed by a partner, but we're still not talking about the fact that sexual assault, and particularly from an early age, affects people's true potential. While we're not having people die from the offending, they're going into adulthood living lives where they're not living to the way they were born to live, so we're having people with comorbidities, mental health, more susceptible to suicide and self-harm, engaging in problematic substance abuse, and trauma as adults.

Here, Rebecca emphasises the importance of providing victim-survivors with coping skills and the first stages of healing as they navigate through a crisis period. Therapeutic work is viewed as an essential and parallel process rather than an afterthought or a distant goal. The deleterious impacts of sexual violence are fully recognised and put on par with non-sexual family violence. Sexual offending may not be an immediate threat to someone's life, but this does not mean it is not life-threatening. Clearly, we cannot afford to lose or water down this service for victims as part of a co-located model. It should also go without saying that embarking on therapeutic work is always up to the victim-survivor. Some may not be ready during a crisis period, and that is okay, but they at least need to have the option to engage in therapeutic work from the outset. Therapeutic services for sexual violence frequently involve long wait times, indicating there is a demand for more to be done in this space.

Another key concern regarding co-located models is the choice of services to integrate. Stakeholders conveyed the importance of responding to the family as a whole unit, to ensure harms against children do not go unnoticed. Child protection services may promote the rights of children, but they can also pose a barrier to women seeking help, especially for First Nations women, who have a fraught history with the forcible removal of their children by government agencies (Langton et al. 2020).

Additionally, co-located family and sexual violence services might encounter the scenario of working with clients who are both victims and perpetrators. For example, a female survivor of family violence might seek services at the same time as a male perpetrator who has a history of child sexual abuse. This is not a stretch to the imagination given the comorbidity of sexual abuse and future perpetration outlined in Chapter 5. Stakeholders who raised this scenario felt that workers would need to be aware of systems abuse (Douglas 2018) to ensure engagement with services was genuine and not part of a perpetrator's broader toolkit of coercive controlling behaviours. They also felt that such situations could be dealt with on a case-by-case basis, and that oversight from leadership and effective communication between services could circumvent systems abuse and promote the safety and well-being of all parties involved in their services.

Other limitations of co-located models are differences in organisational culture and priorities, historical and ongoing competition, inconsistent attendance and participation at meetings, difficulties tracking victims across services, and the potential to confuse or overwhelm victims with too many joint services at the one time (Rizo et al. 2021). Nevertheless, stakeholders report these issues are surmountable, particularly with good leadership that fosters collaboration. For example, counsellor and advocate, Sarah Hill, reported that the success of the co-located centre where she works is aided by a shared ethos between family violence and sexual violence workers, emphasis on teamwork, and social catch-ups outside of work hours to facilitate inter-agency bonding.

The success of any co-located model also lies with funding. As we saw in Chapter 2, politicians are often loath to pay attention to sexual violence and, in turn, funding suffers. Dominant myths about sexual violence persist throughout society; people refuse to believe victim's reports and accept that somebody else (or themselves) could do "that" to another human. Sexual violence services are either lumped together with the family violence budget or left to function on a shoestring. The family violence sector is also underfunded, so it is no wonder that sexual violence services wane if they are merged with family violence services with no additional funding. Adequate funding, equal funding, and agency over funding is the only way of securing the sexual violence sector's autonomy in a co-located approach. The millions of victim-survivors worldwide whose lives and livelihoods are currently under threat deserve to be funded in the same way that government money is thrown at the military.

Cross-pollination and specialism

Co-located or not, there was consensus among our stakeholder interviewees that workers in the family and sexual violence space need core knowledge across both fields to successfully address these harms. The interrelated nature of family violence and sexual offending was well recognised, and stakeholders acknowledged that basic cross-training would be an apt method of boosting understandings, improving collaboration, and, in turn, strengthening responses to the complex web of victim's experiences, ensuring different abuses are not slipping through the cracks. There was also a curiosity and enthusiasm expressed by stakeholders to learn more about the alternate field. This sentiment was captured in discussion with Team Leader, Shureeka Alves:

> I think people are interested and ready to upskill, we're more collaboratively working with these families and really pulling on each other's skills to meet the family's needs. I don't think there's going to be an issue [with shifting identities around work]. I think people are ready for it.

Yet, there was also agreement that we cannot expect everyone to be experts in everything, and by too much cross-training, we run the risk of losing specialism and bombarding workers with more tasks when they are already snowed under. Indeed, the needs of people are manifold, and it would be unrealistic to expect a single case manager to be fully across the nuances of family violence and sexual offending as it pertains to victims, perpetrators, children, adolescents, and adults. This is especially true at a time when many practitioners are feeling burnt out, exacerbated even further by working remotely during the COVID 19 pandemic (Pfitzner, Fitz-Gibbon, & Meyer 2022).

Maintaining specialism is clearly important. Sexual violence in the context of intimate partner relationships is very different to child sexual abuse, stranger sexual violence, elder sexual abuse, and sexual violence in casual dating relationships. While they may share similar underlying drivers and perpetrator tactics, tailored and targeted responses are needed if we are to meaningfully address these harms in different contexts (e.g., sexual consent education in schools and prevention efforts for sexual violence against older people: e.g., Bows 2018). Counsellor and Advocate, Rebecca, also spoke to the benefits of upholding specialism in the diverse therapeutic space of sexual violence work:

> The good thing about being a specialist service in sexual assault is that's all we talk about. We continue to develop best-practice in the space of supporting people who have experienced sexual violence and are committed to updating our trauma-informed response.

This is opposed to generalist psychologists and counsellors who might provide diagnoses and end up engaging in work that is triggering for victim-survivors.

The case for specialism is particularly apparent in policing responses. As elucidated in Chapter 4, the investigation of family violence and sexual offending requires specialist skills, qualities, and fit-for-purpose investigative methodologies that are beyond the scope of general policing. Fast-tracking officers into a specialist command offers a fruitful solution for investigating these crimes, yet it is also essential that frontline officers have basic training and awareness of the dynamics of family and sexual violence. Cases will not be referred onto specialist investigators if frontline responders miss the signs and red flags. This was evident in the U.S. case of Gabby Petito and Brian Laundrie, where frontline officers responded to an incident where a man was seen "slapping a girl." Bodycam footage shows officers laughing and joking with Laundrie and the incident was classified as a mental health episode rather than domestic violence. A month later, Gabby was found dead, with Laundrie ruled responsible for her homicide. While the blame of Gabby's homicide ultimately lies with Laundrie, the case clearly highlighted shortcomings in frontline officers' responses to intimate partner violence, and a need for better police-wide training, particularly given family violence takes up a significant load of police work.

This case, as with many others, also raises questions and implications regarding the initial recruitment of officers. Will officers ever be fit for effective policing work if they hold sexist attitudes and subscribe to myths and misconceptions about family violence and sexual offending? Can we do a better job of screening the right people for the job, prioritising those who already demonstrate empathy, good communications skills, and open-mindedness? These skills and characteristics are important for any policing work, but especially for responding to family and sexual violence (Tidmarsh, Sharman, & Hamilton 2021).

Over the last few decades, we have also seen the gradual move towards specialism at the adjudication phase of the criminal justice process. Specialist courts for family and domestic violence emerged across North America in the 1980s and 1990s and are now widespread across other parts of the world, such as the United Kingdom and Australia. Generally, they have proven to be more effective than traditional courts in terms of case processing, justice outcomes, and victim satisfaction (e.g., Bond et al. 2017; Cook et al. 2004; Cording, Wheatley, & Kaiwai 2021; Scottish Government 2019). Specialist courts for sexual offences, however, are far less common. First appearing in South Africa in 1993, they have received generally positive evaluations over traditional courts (e.g., Flynn 2015; Walker & Louw 2005), but their adoption across other countries has been slow, if at all.

This disparity between the adoption of specialist family violence and sexual offence courts emphasises two issues. Firstly, the lack of dedicated attention and response to sexual violence as a unique and pervasive form of offending in society, highlighted numerous times throughout this book. Secondly, it raises queries of whether there is a need for a separate specialist court for sexual violence or can it be successfully merged with specialist family violence courts? As we now know, there is significant overlap between family violence and sexual offending, but evaluations of specialist family violence courts make seldom mention of their capacity to respond to intimate partner sexual violence, as well as sexual offences outside of familial relationships (Cording et al. 2021; Scottish Government 2019). This is a vital avenue of future research as jurisdictions across the globe continue to trial and rollout specialist courts for family violence and sexual offending.

While we have largely discussed the "horizontal" coordination of agencies to better meet the needs of victim-survivors, Wilcox (2010) has pointed out that "vertical" coordination is needed at every stage of the legal system so that victims have the best chance possible of having their cases understood and addressed in a way that does not create further harm. As discussed in Chapter 5, vertical coordination and cross-pollination of knowledge is particularly important for the family law system, which is so often at odds with specialised understandings of family violence, despite that being a prominent feature of the custody cases they work with. Better training and understandings of the connections between family violence and sexual offending are essential at all points of the civil and criminal law systems so that children and victim-survivors are not left vulnerable to further abuse.

And of course, we are increasingly questioning the suitability of the legal system altogether to deal with any form of family violence and sexual offending. Victim-survivors are avoiding the system in droves and turning to other means of seeking justice, such as restorative justice (CIJ 2014), anonymous online reporting (Loney-Howes, Heydon, & O'Neill 2021), and disclosing abuse online (e.g., O'Neill 2018). Victim-survivors' justice needs are multifaceted and can change over time. Indeed, scholars termed this "kaleidoscopic justice": "a constantly shifting pattern, continually refracted through new experiences and perspectives, with multiple beginnings and no finite ending. Justice as a pluralistic, lived, evolving experience" (McGlynn & Westmarland 2019). It is clear, therefore, that we need a diverse menu of formal and informal justice options for the unique journeys of victim-survivors. In Chapter 6, we argued there are currently more formal options in responses to family violence than sexual offending, however, there is room to develop options for both sectors.

Final words

So why should anyone care about this? Why does any of this matter? In writing this book, many of our friends and family members have been reluctant to discuss family violence and sexual offending. These are clearly uncomfortable topics, but our collective discomfort contributes to the ongoing silence and inaction on these issues. For those that did enquire, there were often misunderstandings or unawareness, which is perhaps not surprising given the common myths about violence and abuse that still permeate society. We were surprised, however, at the curiosity expressed by practitioners and stakeholders. Despite having professional experience and expertise in family violence and/or sexual offending, there were still many question marks, perceived and real unknowns, and an eagerness to teach and learn more about the grey areas presented by these harms.

In trying to bring clarity to these issues, we approached this book with the overarching question of "what is lost and gained when we treat family violence and sexual offending according to the same framework?" In sum, we can gain a more holistic and coordinated approach that recognises the frequent overlapping nature of family and sexual violence. This, in turn, can reflect the reality of many victim-survivors' experiences and prevent disjointed approaches that see victim's needs fall through the cracks. But we risk losing specialism, and as history and research suggests, dedicated attention to sexual offending can fall by the wayside. In moving forward, a more unified approach with efforts to uphold the importance of sexual violence work is needed.

Ultimately, different forms of family violence and sexual offending are all branches on the same tree of patriarchy, misogyny, and gender inequality. They are all part of the same architecture that we need to dismantle, along with specialised efforts to target abuse in various populations and contexts. Whether it is policy language, a prevention campaign, a social or therapeutic service, or a justice response, we need to recognise the relationship between family violence and sexual offending—all the concurring, unique, and nuanced aspects. We like clear categories and lanes, but our responses need to accept the complexity of these problems. In all response efforts, the central tenet should involve listening to victim-survivors' experiences and responding to their individual needs with wraparound care—this should be prioritised above all else.

References

Bilston, G., 2021. *Abuse during sex and degrading porn: This is what sexual coercion can actually look like*. Mamamia, NSW.

Bond, C., Holder, R., Jeffries, J., and Fleming, C., 2017. *Evaluation of the specialist domestic and family violence court trial in Southport: Summary and final report*. Griffith University, Queensland.

Bows, H., 2018. Sexual violence against older people: A review of the empirical literature. *Trauma, Violence, & Abuse, 19*(5), pp. 567–583. doi:10.1177/1524838016683455

CIJ, 2014. *Innovative justice responses to sexual offending – pathways to better outcomes for victims, offenders and the community*. Centre for Innovative Justice RMIT University, Melbourne.

Cook, D., Burton, M., Robinson, A., and Vallely, C., 2004. *Evaluation of specialist domestic violence courts/fast track systems*. Crown Prosecution Service and the Department for Constitutional Affairs, London.

Cording, J., Wheatley, P., and Kaiwai, H., 2021. *Evaluation of the family violence courts*. Ministry of Justice, Aotearoa.

Douglas, H., 2018. Legal systems abuse and coercive control. *Criminology & Criminal justice, 18*(1), pp. 84–99. doi:10.1177/1748895817728380

Flynn, A., 2015. Sexual violence and innovative responses to justice. In A. Powell, N. Henry., & A. Flynn., *Rape justice* (pp. 92–111). Palgrave Macmillan, London.

Koss, M.P., White, J.W., and Lopez, E.C., 2017. Victim voice in reenvisioning responses to sexual and physical violence nationally and internationally. *American Psychologist, 72*(9), p. 1019. doi:10.1037/amp0000233

Langton, M., Smith, K., Eastman, T., O'Neill, L., Cheesman, E., and Rose, M., 2020. *Improving family violence legal and support services for Aboriginal and Torres Strait Islander women*. ANROWS, Sydney.

Loney-Howes, R., Heydon, G., and O'Neill, T., 2021. Connecting survivors to therapeutic support and criminal justice through informal reporting options: An analysis of sexual violence reports made to a digital reporting tool in Australia. *Current Issues in Criminal Justice*, 34(1), pp. 1–18. doi:10.1080/10345329.2021.2004983

Macy, R.J., Giattina, M.C., Montijo, N.J., and Ermentrout, D.M., 2010. Domestic violence and sexual assault agency directors' perspectives on services that help survivors. *Violence against Women, 16*(10), pp. 1138–1161. doi:10.1177/1077801210383085

Macy, R.J., Giattina, M.C., Sangster, T.H., Crosby, C., and Montijo, N.J., 2009. Domestic violence and sexual assault services: Inside the black box. *Aggression and Violent Behavior, 14*(5), pp. 359–373. doi:10.1016/j.avb.2009.06.002

McGlynn, C. and Westmarland, N., 2019. Kaleidoscopic justice: Sexual violence and victim-survivors' perceptions of justice. *Social & Legal Studies, 28*(2), pp. 179–201. doi:10.1177/0964663918761200

O'Neill, T., 2018. 'Today I Speak': Exploring how victim-survivors use reddit. *International Journal for Crime, Justice and Social Democracy*, 7(1), p. 44. doi:10.5204/ijcjsd.v7i1.402

Pfitzner, N., Fitz-Gibbon, K., and Meyer, S., 2022. Responding to women experiencing domestic and family violence during the COVID-19 pandemic: Exploring experiences and impacts of remote service delivery in Australia. *Child & Family Social Work*, *27*(1), pp. 30–40. Doi:10.1111/cfs.12870

Rizo, C.F., Van Deinse, T., Durant, S., Lopez, Q.S., Mason, A., and Ryan, P., 2021. Systematic review of research on co-location models for serving intimate partner and sexual violence survivors. *Journal of Family Violence*, pp.1–19.

Scottish Government., 2019. *Evidence on the effectiveness of integrated domestic abuse courts*. Social Research, Edinburgh.

Tidmarsh, P., Sharman, S., and Hamilton, G., 2021. Police officers' perceptions of specialist training, skills and qualities needed to investigate sexual crime. *Police Practice and Research*, *22*(1), pp. 475–490. doi:10.1080/15614263.2019.1697266

Walker, S.P. and Louw, D., 2005. The court for sexual offences: Perceptions of the victims of sexual offences. *International Journal of Law and Psychiatry*, *28*(3), pp. 231–245. doi:10.1016/j.ijlp.2005.04.001

Wilcox, K., 2010. Connecting systems, protecting victims: towards vertical coordination of Australia's response to domestic and family violence. *University of New South Wales Law Journal*, *33*(3), pp. 1013–1037.

INDEX

www.ingramcontent.com/pod-product-compliance
Ingram Content Group UK Ltd.
Pitfield, Milton Keynes, MK11 3LW, UK
UKHW022018180926
475701UK00005B/913
* 9 7 8 0 3 6 7 5 0 8 8 5 2 *